BOOKS BY LAWRENCE LADER

1955
Margaret Sanger and the Fight for Birth Control

1961
*The Bold Brahmins: New England's War
Against Slavery (1831–1863)*

1966
Abortion

1969
Margaret Sanger: Pioneer of Birth Control
(with Milton Meltzer)

1971
Breeding Ourselves to Death

1972
Foolproof Birth Control: Male and Female Sterilization

1973
Abortion II: Making the Revolution

1979
Power on the Left: American Radical Movements Since 1946

1987
Politics, Power, and the Church

1991
*RU 486: The Pill That Could End the Abortion Wars
and Why American Women Don't Have It*

A
PRIVATE
MATTER

A PRIVATE MATTER: RU 486 AND THE ABORTION CRISIS

LAWRENCE LADER

FOUNDING CHAIR,
NATIONAL ABORTION & REPRODUCTIVE RIGHTS
ACTION LEAGUE

 Prometheus Books

59 John Glenn Drive
Amherst, NewYork 14228-2197

To my wife, Joan Summers Lader,
with love and appreciation.

Published 1995 by Prometheus Books

99 98 97 96 95   5 4 3 2 1

Library of Congress Cataloging-in-Publication Data

Lader, Lawrence.
A private matter : RU 486 and the abortion crisis / Lawrence Lader.
    p.   cm.
    Includes index.
    ISBN 1-57392-012-6 (hardback : alk. paper)
    1. Abortion—Social aspects—United States. 2. Mifepristone (RU 486)—Social aspects—United States. I. Title.
HQ767.5.L32   1995
363.4'6'0973—dc20
                                                                95-20257
                                                                CIP

Printed in the United States of America on acid-free paper

Contents

5

Foreword

by Eleanor Smeal, President, Feminist Majority Foundation

In this era of telephone and electronic communication, we are in danger of losing the history of our movement. The paper trail of letters, books, speeches, and diaries from the early women's movement that fortified our work simply does not exist for this wave of the feminist movement. By losing the legacy of our successes and failures and our knowledge of the forces opposed to women's rights, we condemn the next generation of feminist activists to wasting precious time "recreating the wheel."

A Private Matter rescues the abortion rights movement from this fate. Larry Lader, who has devoted the past thirty years of his life to expanding and preserving women's access to abortion, does a great service to the women's movement. Through his autobiographical discussion of the evolution of the abortion rights movement, Larry describes the leaders, the organizations, and the tactics that launched and sustained it. He makes the movement come alive.

Most importantly, *A Private Matter*—unlike far too many studies of the abortion issue—exposes the opponents of abortion rights. In vivid detail, Larry chronicles the Catholic Church's continuing efforts to deny women their reproductive rights. He documents the tremendous power the Catholic Church wielded in state legislatures as activists worked to repeal laws restricting access to abortions. He

7

describes how the 1975 "Pastoral Plan for Pro-Life Activities" launched the church's questionable electoral involvement, which Abortion Rights Mobilization, under Larry's leadership, challenged in court. He discusses delays in the worldwide distribution of RU 486 when Catholic hospitals threatened to boycott medical products produced by RU 486 manufacturers Hoechst AG and Roussel Uclaf. The Catholic Church's obstructionist role at the 1994 International Conference for Population and Development in Cairo, Egypt, is also outlined.

His account of the history and development of Abortion Rights Mobilization, the organization he founded in 1975, illuminates the difference a small group of committed activists can make in the course of American feminism. The Leona Benten story is a case in point. Larry's brilliantly orchestrated challenge to the Food and Drug Administration's import alert on RU 486 was front-page news across the country and helped galvanize the demands for bringing this medical breakthrough to American women.

Larry Lader continues to be at the forefront of the abortion rights movement. He has remained true to his mentor, Margaret Sanger, in both theory and practice. His uncompromising commitment to women's reproductive rights, his persistence despite significant odds, and his imagination should inspire all of us.

A Private Matter is a call to action for today's activists to preserve the movement's history. This examination of the cutting-edge strategies that have played a role in securing reproductive freedom for women will help guide us in future battles as we move forward in the struggle for women's equality.

1

Causes and Effects in Abortion Rights

Those who become part of a large social movement are changed forever. It is a transformation of overwhelming dimensions. The phone rings constantly. Every detail seems to demand an immediate response. Organizers are pushed from crisis to crisis. Their jobs or professions will never again receive adequate attention. They become persons divided, split into parts, totally obsessed.

This sort of obsession characterized two social movements in American history, movements that changed the way people lived and related to each other and enlarged the advantages of democracy. The first was the anti-slavery movement, which became an organized force in 1831. The second was the abortion rights movement, which started about 1965, as part of the women's movement.

Although slavery was abolished by the Emancipation Proclamation some thirty years later in 1863, the struggle for black equality still torments this century. Abortion rights, by contrast, developed with miraculous speed. When in 1966 my book *Abortion* forced attention on the issue, local groups coalesced into a national movement. In seven years, abortion was legalized through the Supreme Court's *Roe* v. *Wade* decision.[1] Yet the issue is far from settled. The pressure of the opposition has increasingly limited the number of doctors and clinics providing abortion, and rural women have to travel long distances for treatment. Abortion clinic doctors and workers have been threatened or shot; in recent months two doctors, as well as three workers, have been killed. The arrival of RU 486, the French abortion pill, into the United States, promises to relieve the demand for clinical abortions, while at the same time guaranteeing more privacy for women. But RU 486 has become disturbingly controversial, and its introduction overwhelmed by obstacles.

The full story of how the abortion movement started and developed, and how RU 486 has come to play a pivotal role in the struggle, has never been told. I was lucky enough to be an essential part of the movement from the first day. This book presents a personal discussion of how critical decisions were made, how vital strategies were formulated, and how each was carried out. I have tried to probe the passions of the movement and its founders, which is not an easy task. How does one explain how we turned from lawyers and housewives (in my case, from a writer) into frenzied organizers? How did we move from our quiet and secure surroundings to embark upon the dangerous task of offering medically safe yet secret abortions to women years before the laws prohibiting abortion were changed?

What made us decide that the ultimate objective was to bring RU 486 to American women? Often we acted from intuition, yet none of the actions we took would have worked unless every major decision had been grounded in the needs of millions of other people.

Although I was the founding chair of the National Abortion Rights Action League (NARAL) from 1969 to 1975 and president of Abortion Rights Mobilization (ARM) from 1976 to the present, I quickly learned that no officer, no executive committee, can succeed without drawing from a far broader groundswell of public support—an intense fusion of individual determination. Margaret Sanger (1879–1966) and her organizing efforts on behalf of birth control taught us to listen to the deepest yearnings of women. We learned that the desperation of one woman—the primeval search to control her childbearing—undoubtedly mirrored the desperation of countless others.

An idea certainly can be powerful, but real power is achieved when an idea is transformed into tangible action and clearcut results. An idea must have the ability to stir the energies of the multitude. It must be able to inspire local organizing that leads to national organizing, and eventually builds into a national movement.

What drove the early disciples? Many women joined the movement because they had gone through the horrors of an illegal abortion or a relative or friend had gone through it, and they never wanted it to happen to anyone again. The control of their procreation became a towering presence in their lives. Soon it consumed them.

The abolitionist William Lloyd Garrison was once warned by a friend in the 1830s: "Do try to moderate your indignation ... you are all on fire."[2] We had to be on fire when we were building the abortion rights movement. We had to give ourselves completely to something far bigger than our daily concerns. We knew that with each step, whether referring a woman secretly to a doctor for abortion or organizing a local abortion rights chapter, we were achieving something concrete. It gave our lives meaning and direction.

It also provided a sense of power. When we helped guide a new abortion rights law through a state legislature or constructed a test case in the courts that expanded feminist rights, we experienced the exhilaration of knowing that we were pushing the country forward. We were creating a momentum we were sure could not be stopped. We were part of an adventure that was changing society.

The daily grind of expanding the movement and keeping up the pressure for reforms, as well as the perpetual crises, soon took their toll. Many of the early veterans suffered burnout and disappeared: one lawyer not only gave up the law but retreated to a monastic hideout where he supported himself with menial jobs. I suspect my survival was due to pure stubbornness, imprisoned by the conviction that I shouldn't start a project unless I could see it through to the end. I may also have been glad to escape from a writer's lonely shell, plunging into a world of action and passion, constantly buoyed by my interaction with others even if it meant I was torn between two lives.

The most impressive aspect of the abortion rights movement is the speed with which it swept the country. Movements are mysterious, depending on a host of factors that must converge at the same time. Abortion rights surfaced at a propitious moment. Although abortion had been legal under English common law and by extension in the thirteen American colonies, it was virtually wiped out after the Civil War for a period of a hundred years. The demand for increasing population with westward expansion and booming industry placed a moral stigma on abortion. The medical profession claimed to be protecting women's health against what were claimed to be crude abortion techniques performed by even the best doctors, and it was equally eager to make women subservient by blocking birth control as well as abortion.

Then everything changed in the early 1960s as the National Organization for Women (NOW) and other feminist groups empowered women with the vision that the ability to have control over their own bodies through abortion was a basic right, as was controlling every part of their lives. Other factors added to the new freedom women sought. The safety and efficiency of abortion was guaranteed by the development of antibiotics and a simple, new technique known as vacuum abortion, which replaced surgical instruments with a pump that drew out fetal tissues. Legalized abortion in Japan, the former Soviet Union, Eastern Europe, and eventually Great Britain provided the final, supportive force that gave the abortion movement an international impetus.

Although abortion was still the "dread secret of society," the Supreme Court's decision in *Griswold* v. *Connecticut*[3] (1965) offered constitutional validity by enlarging the scope of an individual's right to privacy in sexual matters. The decision concerned birth control, but its interpretation of privacy and family planning rights was so broad that I insisted in the last chapter of my book, *Abortion,* published in 1966, that it could be applied to abortion as well as contraception.

In delivering the opinion of the Court, Justice William O. Douglas ruled that the Fourth and Fifth Amendments protected against governmental invasion of privacy and concluded that

"The present case, then, concerns a relationship lying within the zone of privacy created by several fundamental constitutional guarantees." In his concurring opinion, Justice Arthur J. Goldberg, joined by Chief Justice Earl Warren and Justice William J. Brennan, Jr., declared that "The right of marital privacy is protected as being within the protected penumbra of specific guarantees of the Bill of Rights," and concluded that the right to privacy is "a personal right 'retained by the people' within the meaning of the Ninth Amendment."

Today the abortion rights movement is thirty years old. Generations of younger people have replaced its veterans. When half a million men and women poured into Washington, D.C., in 1989 for the National March for Women's Equality/Women's Lives, it seemed assured that feminist power had become one of the dominant political blocs in the country. Yet by 1995, some critics were insisting the movement was in decline. Scattered objectives such as the antipornography movement were draining its concentration. The monolithic strength of the Catholic and Protestant fundamentalist churches was exhausting feminist financial resources.

Can the abortion rights movement maintain its militancy? The immediate test is whether abortion services will be incorporated into any new health care plan emerging from Capitol Hill. Never ceasing to attack abortion as "murder," the right wing has diverted attention from the legal abortion clinics to a campaign against homosexuals, sex education, and condom distribution in schools.

Historic parallels give us ample warning. When constitutional amendments after the Civil War guaranteed former slaves their full standing as citizens, the abolitionists were convinced that their objectives had been won. Although a few took government posts in the South or taught at black schools, most receded into anonymity. Few protested when federal troops were withdrawn from the rebel states in 1876, leaving these states to legislate a new version of slavery with segregation laws.

Anti-abortionists today are counting on the same political upheavals. Even with congressional legislation and court decisions which supposedly diminish the possibility of abortion clinics being attacked, five clinics were fire-bombed in less than a month in February and March of 1995.[4] Extremists know that the chances of a Republican president in 1996, along with a Republican Congress, could seriously weaken the abortion rights movement.

Despite these threats, the women's movement has already changed our lives and will continue to do so. The right of a woman to control her body and to exercise her procreation options is basic to all women's aims. A woman cannot achieve the education she wants unless she has the right to plan her childbearing. She cannot embark on a job or career unless a child is planned to meet her personal growth. She cannot have a fulfilling home life unless she and her partner can have a child that they want at the time that they want.

It is not just the militants in NOW or other organizations who are affected. The contemporary roles men play in society—whether in the office or as housekeepers or fathers—have been drastically reshaped. Economic pressures have been a major factor. As the two-income family has become essential to maintaining a necessary standard of living, men who formerly expected their wives to be adornments and childraisers, always at their command, now depend on their partners to contribute a substantial share, often the dominant share, of the household income. One obvious example is the Mormon church, which had always limited women to the roles of breeder and home-maker. Today an increasing number of Mormon women hold jobs and are essential to the economic survival of their men.[5]

It has become clear that the women's movement (and many other movements, such as those which seek to affect environmental change or gun control) are far more decisive in molding our lives than most congressional or White House programs. Except for occasional, monumental legislation, such as the Social Security Act under President Franklin D. Roosevelt, the legislative and executive branches of government too rarely touch the way Americans struggle to achieve their personal needs.

Political parties no longer provide the most direct route toward gaining women's aspirations. Important as it is to elect women to local and national office, the most effective road to change has been pursued by social movements whose members can achieve their ends, not just through electing political leaders, but through pressure groups, court cases, picket lines, marches, and other activist approaches.

Safeguarding abortion rights must be considered the dominant objective of the women's movement. Although help has come from Congress and the president through Freedom of Access to Clinic Entrances (FACE)[6] legislation, which establishes federal protection against violent demonstrations, the law mainly resulted from feminist lobbying. Importantly, many Republicans joined Democrats in its passage. (Please see appendix for a copy of the entire FACE law.)

The long-term responsibility for abortion rights, however, falls on the women's movement. Since federal marshals and police can't be everywhere they are needed to escort patients, the women's movement will have to supply guards around the clinics; escort patients, doctors, and staff members safely from their homes to the clinics; and make sure that staff members' homes are protected. Above all, it is up to the movement to convince medical schools to train more young doctors in abortion techniques, and recruit them to work at clinics that have been targeted for bombings and shootings.

The second objective of the women's movement is that the medical availability of the drug RU 486 must be considered essential to maintaining a woman's right to abortion nationwide. RU 486 acts on the body's hormone-receiving tissues or receptors (a different receptor for each hormone). It induces abortion by causing the uterus to shed its lining much like a monthly period. Many women prefer this chemical method to intrusive surgery. It gives them control of their own abortion. Moreover, RU 486 will introduce a wide sphere of privacy. The pills can be dispensed either at a clinic or at a doctor's private office with the physician monitoring the results.

Prescribing RU 486 will maintain the same doctor-patient relationship that accompanies the use of an antibiotic or any drug. It will be virtually impossible for enemies of abortion to pinpoint an administering doctor or picket every medical office in the country. The use of RU 486 should also become increasingly common in rural areas where few clinics exist, and diminish the need for women to travel long distances for surgical abortions.

No prediction can be made as to how many American

women will prefer RU 486 to the vacuum method. In France, about half of all patients request it. In Britain, the percentage is less, possibly because the national health system is structured around hospitals favoring the vacuum method. In my judgment, the American demand will be equal to that of France. Abortion Rights Mobilization (ARM), the group I head, has staked all its efforts in recent years on this outcome, and worked extensively to get RU 486 to American women quickly.

If we are right in our assessment of the demand, the clinic system of abortion should not be radically affected. The need for vacuum abortion will keep most clinics in operation. But clinics will also become part of a referral network, sending women requesting RU 486 to doctors on their list who administer the pill in their own offices.

Although this concentration on RU 486 may be a gamble, almost every important strategy since the movement started has been an equal gamble. This book will analyze the early days of abortion rights to compare past strategies to the present campaign for the pill. It will conclude that the mounting pressure on clinics through assassinations and firebombings, as well as heightened anti-abortion sentiment in Congress, makes it essential to guarantee the privacy of all women.

Privacy is the key to the future; it inextricably links RU 486 to the women's movement. It is the thesis of this book that the success of each depends on the success of the other.

NOTES

1. *Roe* v. *Wade,* 410 U.S. 113 (1973).

2. Quotation by Samuel J. May from May, *Some Recollections of Our Antislavery Conflict,* Fields, Osgood, Boston, 1869.

3. *Griswold* v. *Connecticut,* 381 U.S. 479 (1965).

4. *New York Times,* March 3, 1995, p. A 16.

5. *Time Magazine,* July 29, 1991, p. 22; *What the 1990 Census Tells Us About Women,* Population Reference Bureau, Washington, D.C., November 1993, p. 83.

6. "Freedom of Access to Clinic Entrances Act of 1994," Public Law 103-259, 103rd Congress, 2nd Session, 103 P.L. 259, 108 Stat. 694, 1994 Enacted S 636, 103 Enacted S. 636.

2

The Sanger Factor

Every soldier in the Pacific was obsessed with the slogan, "Golden Gate in '48." We expected the war to last until 1948. I boarded a troop ship to the States three years ahead of time, arriving in San Francisco in February 1945, a five-stripe sergeant bound for Officers Candidate School, but destined to return for the final assault on Japan.

When the graceful arc of the Golden Gate bridge finally appeared out of the mist, we cheered and pounded the rails with our canteens like mad men. Red Cross women poured us coffee on the dock. We hugged and kissed them, wanting only the brief touch of warm bodies that we had dreamed about for years.

Once I got into San Francisco, I searched for a newsstand and bought a copy of the *New Yorker*. In it was my own article, my own byline, my "Letter from New Caledonia" that I had scrawled so laboriously in my tent at night. All those army years shaved off my career had now been paid back. I had been published by the magazine that every writer longed to crack.

On August 6, 1945, a week or so before we would be com-

missioned second lieutenants, I was celebrating my twenty-
sixth birthday with a keg of beer I had bought for the platoon.
Someone rushed into the barracks with news that had come ·
over the radio. A strange bomb had been dropped on Hiroshima
and virtually wiped out the city. No one had heard of it or
understood it. But as we listened to the radio, the horror of this
incalculable new weapon gradually gave way to a feeling of
selfishness and even rejoicing. In one burst of devastation,
turning a Japanese city to cinders, our own lives had been
secured. There were no cheers, but it was obvious we would not
be going to the Pacific and the war would soon be over.

Everyone seemed to be making up for lost time in those first
months after the war. Even on rainy days, the streets were
bathed in splendor. I raced everywhere as if the illusion of freedom around each corner was too ephemeral to trust. I wore my
hat at a cocky angle. The girls were no longer pinups on a
Pacific tent wall, but goddesses waiting to be brought to earth
and enveloped. The *Esquire/Coronet* offices, where I had been
hired as contributing editor, overflowed with seduction.

I was divorced now after a wartime marriage to a childhood
sweetheart that had little more going for it than habit and polite-
ness. The managing editor's secretary was blonde and tall and
partial to dresses that hardly kept each curve in place. Because
our magazines received second night seats to Broadway shows,
Mary started inviting me to escort her. She would often stay
overnight at my apartment, telling her mother in an era when
twenty-one-year-olds still lived at home that she had to work
late and couldn't get back to Long Island.

When we decided to spend a week in June at Gloucester,
Massachusetts, Mary concocted a visit to a former classmate

living nearby. As we set off in my car, we stopped at a jewelry store on Sixth Avenue to buy a dollar wedding band, a totem we thought necessary at a New England resort.

The Thorwald was a huge wooden pile above the beach, built a century before and crowded with Harvard professors and Beacon Hill dowagers who had made it their second home. Mary and I were not just unique for our youth, but when she entered the dining room on my arm, her once-ivory skin bronzed by the sun, her body sheathed in white, the diners seemed to leap from their seats and devour us with hungry eyes. It was good to be young and a survivor in 1946. My class at Harvard had suffered the highest casualty rate in history, and I had lost many close friends in the war.

In the glittering crescendo of those postwar years, I moved from affair to affair. Vacationing in Rome after magazine assignments in Europe, I met a married woman from New York, rich and from a prominent family, which may have added to the lure of her voluptuousness. It was impossible to resist her in that Roman cocoon thousands of miles from reality, the caress of her fingers in my palm at the opera, the panting embraces under the cedars on the moon-dappled benches of Borghese Park.

In New York, when she came to my apartment, she warned me that a jealous husband had put detectives on her track. Such obstacles only heightened the excitement. We went to galleries together as she added paintings to her collection. She gave me an exotic bowl, and I gave her John Donne's poems, which we read in bed.

In the next few years, I was determined to build a reputation in the magazine profession, writing regularly for *Look, Col-*

lier's, Reader's Digest, New Republic, and most of the important journals. I wrote on the scandal of our county jails and on union organizing in the feudal empires of the textile-mill South. I became something of a specialist in the treatment of emotionally ill children and the possibility of early detection and treatment of mental illness. I wrote frequent profiles on such vivid figures as Alfred Lunt, Lynn Fontanne, Carl Sandburg, and Mae West. I was producing twelve or more long pieces a year, often at my desk from nine in the morning till midnight, pushing myself to exhaustion.

All this time I was looking for a book subject that would not only make exciting reading, but that would involve meaningful currents of social change. I would sit in the public library at 42nd Street for days, scanning the *Times Index* for subject ideas, thumbing through news magazines and drawers of file cards. It has always been my belief that nothing is really accidental. The groundwork generally leads in an inescapable direction. The mind is tuned to certain needs, and waits only for an impelling force to set off an explosion long ready to burst.

While there was no such thing as a feminist movement in 1952, I had always been aware of its possibility. In my early marriage, my wife had come out of a radical group at Vassar that saw itself pushing towards a new status for women. My wife was set on a career. She worked in radio and at the Office of War Information. She kept her maiden name on the job and on the door of our apartment. She had her own bank account. All these steps were rare in that era.

When I entered left-wing politics with the American Labor party, I worked with women who never accepted a secondary role, but became district leaders and campaign managers and often had scores of men under their command. I not only enjoyed being in love with these women, I liked their company and I relished their initiative and individuality.

I was looking for a new type of woman, one who would break out of all the prejudices and molds of the past.

In my search for a book subject, in 1952, something stirred my deepest instincts when I came across the name of Margaret Sanger, the birth control pioneer; here was an extraordinary example of the "New Woman." Her vision was earthshaking. Her ability to turn an idea into a social movement was unique. Her message—that through birth control, women could consciously plan the direction of their lives and raise themselves to a new level of dignity—was already stamped on this century. Best of all she was alive and still organizing. "When the history of our civilization is written," H. G. Wells said, "it will be a biological history and Margaret Sanger will be its heroine."[1]

I was amazed to find that as far back as 1914, in the first issue of her magazine *Woman Rebel,* she had proclaimed that "A woman's body belongs to herself alone."[2] She quickly understood that until women broke out of "biological slavery," as she called it, and could control their own childbearing, all other feminist needs—the vote, education, jobs—were peripheral. She saw women's lives broken by unwanted, incessant pregnancies. Only birth control, she argued, could give women immediate equality.

Birth control could benefit children as well as mothers. "The first right of every child," she insisted, "is to be wanted, to be desired, to be planned with an intensity of love that gives it its title to being."[3]

Sanger quickly rebelled against the social and religious

dogma of the Victorian era. Her father, Michael Higgins, was an Anglo-Irish freethinker. When he invited Robert Ingersoll, a propagandist for agnosticism, to speak at their prudish hometown of Corning, New York, Higgins was locked out of the hall, owned by the Catholic church but already rented and paid for. Sanger would battle similar church censorship throughout her career.

Margaret's mother, Anne Purcell, was a devout Catholic who gave birth to eleven children. Sanger saw how endless childbearing destroyed her mother's health and led to her early death. "I can never look back on my childhood with joy," she wrote years later. "Even when I'm passing through Corning at night by train . . . I actually become sick to my stomach."

Working as a nurse in New York City in 1912, Sanger was horrified by the poverty of the Lower East Side, where forty families were often crowded into sixteen apartments. She recognized the link between poverty and unwanted children. When women pleaded with doctors and nurses to tell them how to prevent another child, they were ignored. The Comstock law passed by Congress in 1873, as well as its New York State equivalent, forbade dissemination of contraceptive materials or advice. Sanger decided to challenge the laws head-on, describing the known methods of contraception in *Family Limitation,* published in 1914. On August 25th that year she was indicted and fled to England to prepare her defense and rally support.

Her reactions were always blunt and flamboyant. After opening the first birth control clinic in Brooklyn, New York, in 1916, she was arrested and jailed for thirty days. Still, she struggled for hours against being fingerprinted by the police, insisting that running a clinic did not put her in the same category as "common" criminals.[4]

Her struggle was not only against the Catholic church and its Victorian restrictions against sex, but against the medical profession. As late as 1925, Dr. Morris Fishbein, editor of the *Journal of the American Medical Association,* insisted that no birth control technique was "physiologically, psychologically, and biologically sound in both principle and practice." By converting prominent doctors and opening a network of clinics across the country, Sanger eventually overturned medical opposition.

Far ahead of her time, Sanger made population control an international issue in 1922 when she warned that Japanese overpopulation abetted the aims of the militarists by providing more bodies for war and causing economic instability. In 1959, a Presidential commission finally acknowledged her vision, and urged that "stabilizing the growth of the world's population" become official, U.S. policy.[5] President Eisenhower, who had rejected the report six years earlier, now backed it.

Shortly after she agreed to work with me on her biography, published in 1955 as "The Margaret Sanger Story," she told me, "You must always be in love. Life is meaningless unless you are in love."

Margaret Sanger was the greatest influence on my life. Our relationship remains hard to define even today. She was seventy-four when we met, I was thirty-four. There was never anything physical between us, but she insisted that I stay close to her constantly. In Tucson, Arizona, I slept at the house of a friend of hers a few blocks from Sanger's residence, yet she had me spending all day and evening with her. It was the same in Santa Barbara, California, and in Stowe, Vermont. At first I thought it was simply loneliness, for she occasionally referred to her home as the "Well of Loneliness." But soon I suspected there was something more. She would pour out intimate memories late at night, then seem to regret the torture of exploring the past and complain in a note, "You must have had a magic wand." When we began to exchange letters, almost every letter was filled with endearments.

There was a vague resemblance to courtships to be sure. But on her part, there was mainly a desire to win me to her views so that I could better write about the movement. I was obviously flattered by an intimate link to this heroic figure, but I also wanted to come as close as possible to my own concept of the "New Woman," and test my beliefs against the example of one who had created a movement from her own willpower and offered it to the world.

Her doctrines shaped my future writing and campaigns on birth control and abortion. Sanger opposed abortion—she was horrified after watching large numbers of poor women line up on Saturday nights outside the offices of quack abortionists during her nursing days in New York. But she stirred my thinking by making me read the one medical text on the subject. I agonized over abortion for years, increasingly convinced that contraception alone could never handle the problem of unwanted pregnancies; that the horrors of back-alley abortion must be stopped and the procedure performed safely in hospitals and clinics. When I published the first book calling for legalization of abortion in 1966, and became overnight a campaigner rather than a writer, it was as though every step I made was with Margaret Sanger's ghost at my side, directing my strategy.

NOTES

1. H. G. Wells, from his speech at London dinner, 1935, reprinted in *Round the World for Birth Control* (1937), in Sanger collection, Smith College.

2. Only a few issues of *Woman Rebel* were published from March to August, 1914, when Sanger was arrested. One set is at the Library of Congress, Washington, D.C.

3. See also Margaret Sanger, *Woman and the New Race,* Truth Publishing Co., New York, 1929, pp. 1, 94, 228.

4. For this and prior pars. on Sanger, see Lawrence Lader, *Margaret Sanger and the Fight for Birth Control,* Doubleday, New York, 1955, pp. 13–16, 45–49, 107–16.

5. Lader, op. cit. pp. 311, 320–21, 326–29, 342–43. Quotations from Sanger are from author's interviews with her from 1953 to 1955.

3

Launching an Idea: Abortion Rights

A deeply disturbing book, *An Essay on the Principle of Population* by the Reverend Thomas Malthus, was published in England in 1798. It presented an ominous thesis on population growth. Backed by the application of mathematics to the statistical records of previous centuries, Malthus warned that the burgeoning number of inhabitants on the planet would soon outnumber the supply of food, natural resources, and other essential items.

Malthus was either ridiculed or ignored. In an era of exuberant industrial growth, combined with the glittering conquests of the British empire, Britain's wars demanded ever-increasing manpower. Its Industrial Revolution required child labor for its factories.

In the next decades, Malthus gathered only a few lonely disciples, and those who suggested rudimentary forms of contraception often ended up in jail as enemies of public morality. It was not until 1876 that the Malthusian movement gained any acceptance in Britain, strangely enough, through the notorious trial of a publisher.

Charles Knowlton's book, *The Fruits of Philosophy,* attracted only a few American readers in 1832 with its description of crude methods of contraception and its analysis of the impact of excessive childbearing on maternal health. However, these "immoral" subjects led to Knowlton's arrest and three months at hard labor in an East Cambridge, Massachusetts, jail.

Virtually forgotten in America except among a few advocates of women's rights such as Victoria Claflin Woodhull, Knowlton's book became the Bible of the tiny Malthusian movement in England. In 1876, a Bristol publisher was arrested for selling it. To make this a clearcut case of the infringement of the rights of free press, Charles Bradlaugh, a Malthusian and radical Member of Parliament, and his partner and lover, Annie Besant, published their own edition of the book and were promptly arrested.

The trial, held before the Lord Chief Justice on the Court of Queen's Bench, dominated the headlines of every British newspaper. Bradlaugh and Besant conducted their own defense. Convicted at first of destroying public morals, they appealed to a higher court and won. Still, Bradlaugh was denied his seat in Parliament. He went back to his district and was reelected, a charade that continued from 1880 until 1886, with Bradlaugh often administering the oath of office to himself. The speaker of Parliament finally agreed to seat him.

The trial had many repercussions. It established in England that contraception was no longer to be considered an obscenity. It focused attention on Malthusian principles. Between Bradlaugh's and Besant's arrest and trial, *Fruits of Philosophy* sold 125,000 copies, after the trial another 185,000, and at least 50,000 in other editions.

Malthusian principles were gradually being pushed in the United States by radicals such as Robert Ingersoll and John H. Noyes at the Oneida community in upper New York State, which required birth control of its members. Margaret Sanger was introduced to Malthus through Havelock Ellis, the English psychologist already famed for his seven-volume *Psychology of Sex.*

In America as well as Britain, new forces were emerging, particularly in the middle and upper middle classes. With improved medical care and the decline in infant mortality, the more affluent wanted better education and a higher standard of living for their children. Birth rates dropped sharply. In 1912, Margaret Sanger began a campaign that would make birth control an accepted technique for most women. Sanger generally ignored male contraception in order to keep responsibility in women's hands.

But even with fewer children among industrialized nations, the underdeveloped world began increasing its birth rates. The earth's population doubled and redoubled just as Malthus had predicted.

By the 1960s poverty, famine, and disease had become an international disaster, and President John Kennedy convinced Congress to allocate funds for overseas contraceptive assistance. It took 160 years, but Malthus's ideas at last were vindicated. Population control was accepted as American policy.

In reviewing the history of ideas, it seemed to me that the truly great ideas had to be rooted in the needs of society. They had to come at the right time, when social forces were primed and ready to support them.

One striking example was the development of the American

antislavery movement. Despite its tumultuous campaigning, it never achieved a widespread base in the North until other social forces caught the public's attention. In 1848, the new Free Soil party cut into the vote of both major parties with its rabid opposition to the spread of slavery into northern territories. Open warfare over a free or slave Kansas would prove the Union was at risk.

A new and critical factor was the emergence of the Republican party in 1856, uniting the antislavery and free soil movements. The issue now involved economic issues as well as moral issues, as northern financiers and businessmen saw that the country's destiny lay in the undeveloped West. Financiers like John Murray Forbes were building cross-country railroad lines. Textile magnates like Amos A. Lawrence poured money and guns into free-soil colonization of Kansas. They may have opposed slavery, but their main concern—embodied in the Republican party—was to control the West. In this fusion with large and small business, the antislavery movement finally put together a popular base.

In 1950, when I was thirty years old, I was involved in developing an idea that would have an impact on society. I was doing a lot of magazine writing on urban problems, and often researched at the National Municipal League in New York, a foundation devoted to city management. Exploring an article, I stumbled across a file on Moore County, Tennessee, where a mere 3,454 people in one district elected a House member to the state legislature, whereas in the Shelby county district it took 78,000 people to elect a single House member.

This meant that one vote in Moore had roughly twenty-three times the power of one vote in Shelby, an unequal pattern repeated throughout Tennessee. More research uncovered a similar problem in Connecticut and half the states in the country. These voting districts had usually been established roughly 100 years earlier—Connecticut hadn't reapportioned its districts since 1818—and were never adjusted to meet the growth of city populations and the decline of rural populations.

It made a sad commentary on the democratic principle of equal representation.

Magazines were eager then for this kind of scandal, and I placed the article with *This Week,* a Sunday supplement in hundreds of newspapers. The article got a lot of attention in nationwide editorials, and *This Week* booked me on frequent talk shows. While I had obviously hit on something big, I never thought about turning the idea into a campaign that would change the political system. I was just a young writer, concentrating on establishing a reputation in a highly competitive profession. Nothing was further from my thinking than becoming a reformer.

At last my article caught the attention of radio station WMCA in New York City, which decided that the problem was so critical that the station would wage a campaign for legislative reapportionment. Other broadcasters and media were drawn to the campaign and soon the public was aware of a scandal that denied millions of people their voting rights.

Now it would take legislative and legal experts to find a technique for action. The key movers turned out to be the Citizens Committee for Reapportionment in Tennessee, which included Martin Ochs, editor of the *Chattanooga Times* and a member of the influential Ochs family, which owned the *New York Times*. The committee brought a lawsuit in federal court under the "equal protection" clause of the Fourteenth Amendment. Because the Constitution guaranteed that no one can be denied equal rights that are secured to others, the U.S. Supreme Court logically would be concerned about millions of citizens whose votes had only a tenth or a thirtieth of the impact of their neighbors' votes.

Rendering its opinion on March 26, 1962, the Supreme Court ruled that every state legislative district must contain approximately the same population as other districts, and gave federal courts power to enforce reapportionment.[1] It had taken a decade to bring about a political revolution, but it was a striking example of the importance of an idea. What had seemed to me simply a magazine article, buried too long in the files of the Municipal League, had grown over the years into a groundswell of public opinion that had become the law of the land.

I decided to begin my first book in 1952, the biography of Margaret Sanger, a tireless pioneer of birth control whose struggle against legal, social, and moral prejudice had produced a chain of contraceptive clinics across the country. She had moved against walls of ignorance and toppled them. Her dominant teaching—that the health and stability of the family could only be ensured when every child was a wanted child—became my credo too.

I began to question Sanger about abortion. Sanger's whole campaign was based on the premise that birth control could eliminate the danger of abortion. Ironically, she rarely took into account the possibility that every birth control technique had an inherent failure rate or could fail through misuse. Once we went to a film based on Theodore Dreiser's *An American Tragedy,* whose plot hinged on the repercussions of an unwanted pregnancy. "That girl could never have become pregnant if birth control had been accepted then," Sanger insisted.

Further, Sanger never did grasp the medical advances in abortion. The introduction of the vacuum suction technique from China and the use of antibiotics against infection had virtually eliminated risk. By the 1950s, abortion was safe and efficient if performed by a physician.

By moving from contraception to abortion, I was essentially in conflict with Sanger, and this often disturbed me. I was also entertaining an area ignored by Betty Friedan, the most aggressive neo-feminist of that period, and a friend from my ex-wife's circle in 1941. Strangely, Friedan had overlooked Sanger's teachings. Her book *The Feminist Mystique,* published in 1963, had only three short references to Sanger, none to contraception, none to abortion. The only explanation is that women had not yet emerged from the straitjacket of sexual taboos that society had clamped on them. "We were afraid of being called 'loose women' if we talked about abortion," one feminist said. "I was so obsessed with the issue of equality that I couldn't face the meaning of sex," Friedan told me.

It was undoubtedly odd for me to be haunted by the subject of abortion, which was considered unmentionable in 1962. It not only set me against the Catholic church and many other religious groups; it conflicted with the deepest sexual taboos of our culture. Abortion was a forbidden word, too dangerous to touch. Many newspaper and broadcasting stations refused to mention the subject. To advocate the right of abortion meant tearing down what was considered a wall against immorality. For both the single and the married woman it meant destroying the ultimate punishment for engaging in sex for its own sake—the obligation of childbirth.

The Puritan tradition linked sex with evil and guilt. Laws

against contraception and abortion were intended to degrade women. The male-dominated world assumed that a woman would be terrified to indulge in sex when pregnancy would expose her "sin." Abortion thus stood at the apex of our inhibitions. Tampering with it might mean that the whole system could come tumbling down.

All this seemed completely irrational to me. For the state to force any woman to bear a child against her will was a brutal abuse of her personal liberty. I was angered by any attempt to enforce morality by law. If contraception failed or was misused, or even if it was never used, why shouldn't women have the right to control their childbearing through abortion? Why had abortion become such an unspeakable crime?

The more I researched the subject at the New York Academy of Medicine, the more I realized the injustice of America's punitive laws. Abortion before "quickening"—when the fetus moved in the womb—had long been legal, under English common law, in our colonial courts, and in the U.S. court system until just before the Civil War. Prohibitive state laws were partly intended to protect women against the crude abortion techniques, even by doctors, in that era.[2]

Another motivation of these laws was the Victorian obsession with sin. The federal Comstock Act of 1873 enabled Anthony Comstock of the New York Society for the Suppression of Vice to close down the city's most prominent abortionist, who had practiced without interference from her Fifth Avenue mansion ever since 1838.[3]

Even the Catholic church had never punished abortion as murder before a soul became rational or "animated"—forty days after conception for a male fetus, about eighty days for a female fetus, although theologians never explained how the sex of the fetus would be determined. The animation theory was not abandoned by the Vatican until 1869, when all abortion was considered murder.

The blanket of secrecy around the subject was only lifted for a few days in 1962 in the case of Sherri Finkbine, a television hostess at an Arizona station. She had taken the drug thalidomide, then prescribed as a tranquilizer, for nervous exhaustion and chest pains. Shortly after she began to take the drug, Ms. Finkbine found herself pregnant. Newspapers nationwide carried reports that thalidomide could severely damage a fetus.

Ms. Finkbine sought abortion at a local hospital that agreed to help, but soon reversed its decision. Finkbine and her husband frantically flew to Sweden, which approved abortion for this indication. The hospital announced that the fetus was indeed deformed—"It was not a baby," the doctor said.[5]

It was absurd that a woman had to leave the United States for proper medical treatment. It seemed equally odd that abortion should still be illegal even when the reason for such laws had become obsolete. The dangers of an abortion had been eliminated. Victorian morality was scarcely in vogue a century after the Comstock Act. The nineteenth-century demand for larger population had been replaced by the increasing acceptance of birth control and of smaller families.

I was gradually working toward a major idea: that abortion was as much a right as birth control and that all antiquated and punitive abortion laws should be abolished. The idea terrified me. It appeared the height of folly that a lone writer should try to overthrow a system that had been in place for a century. A

article, would plunge me into a maelstrom of
ig into the few flamboyant memoirs by abor-
;azine articles on the subject. There had never
been a well-researched treatment of American abortion, or even
a whisper that the laws should be abolished.

For years I debated with myself, testing every approach on
my wife to make sure my thinking was both reasonable and
defensible. Even if English common law could be pointed to
when supporting abortion before quickening, could you support
it at four months or six months when the fetus approached viability? Should the state have the power to intervene in abortion?
If so, at what stage of pregnancy?

The basic discovery of my research was that the law only
accepted the child as a human person *after* the infant had
emerged from the womb. If the fetus was not a person in legal
terms, I decided that the state, and certainly religion, should
have less power over incipient life than the mother herself.

This was the biggest leap in my thinking. A fetus was part
of a woman's body. A woman's decision over childbearing is
therefore paramount. Although the state might have some
claims in late pregnancy, I shaped my conclusion in personal
terms. If my wife had faced a decision in late abortion as a
result of fetal damage, an auto accident or other similar physical or mental trauma, I hoped she would consult not only me,
but a physician. Yet the ultimate decision must rest with my
wife. Only a woman should be in total control of her body and
of childbearing. No state, organized religion, or outside agency
should interfere. I then made the ultimate step in my thinking:
all laws that restricted a woman's right to abortion must be
abolished immediately.

Later I was forced to find constitutional grounds to back up my beliefs. Although the Supreme Court had rendered many decisions on aspects of privacy, the crucial decision was in the case of *Griswold* v. *Connecticut* in 1965, overthrowing the state's power to limit the sale and distribution of contraceptives. As I mentioned earlier, the Court's language seemed so encompassing that I felt I could make one more leap and apply it to abortion as well.

In my book *Abortion* I would later deduce from *Griswold:*

> Since the Court laid such emphasis on rights retained by the people, it might well be asked whether abortion does not fall within this category. . . . abortion as well as marital privacy deserves the protection of the Constitution.[6]

These were daring words, based on the assumption that because contraception and abortion both gave a woman control over her childbearing, they should be treated equally under the law. It would turn out to be sound reasoning. In legalizing abortion in 1973, the Court essentially adopted the same argument.

As I worked through the early obstacles in 1962, I despaired of my ability to turn what state laws called a crime into a woman's right. When I decided to write a magazine outline and then submitted it to seven or eight editors, most of whom I knew socially as well as professionally, they all rejected it. I was beginning to worry that association with the subject could damage my career and perhaps make me an outcast.

Still, I liked challenges. From the time I had been a volunteer district leader (from 1946 to 1950) for Congressperson Vito Marcantonio, the most radical member of the House, I had

had a penchant for conflict. I may have even liked the challenge—although never equating myself with Margaret Sanger—of doing battle against the authoritarianism of the Catholic church.

Deep in my subconscious, I suspect, I welcomed identification with a feminist cause. Abortion rights may have been ignored or maligned, but a book advocating these rights could put me in the vanguard of feminism, a pioneering role I thought I would enjoy.

If a man took part in a woman's agonizing search for abortion, he was, in effect, intervening in a critical point in her life. I often examined these motivations later, when I was referring some two thousand women to doctors performing abortions quietly in their offices during the illegal era. Naturally, I was eager to help them. But even with the risk of my arrest, I realized that, briefly, I was part of the crisis that each woman was going through.

Whatever my motives, I plunged on. If I failed to sell an article, I would write a book. Again my outline was rejected by two or three publishers until at last the Bobbs-Merrill company signed me to a contract. Writing the book took three years of grinding work. For research on abortion in Europe and Japan, the late Dr. Christopher Tietze at the National Committee on Maternal Health was a source of my statistics. In the United States, except for Dr. Alfred Kinsey's book, and a few primitive studies, I had to find women who would talk about their own abortions, doctors who would risk describing their referrals, and abortionists who were frank about their arrests and imprisonments.

My principal help came from Dr. William Ober, a prominent pathologist and college classmate, who joined me in developing a detailed questionnaire on abortion that was sent to thousands of obstetrician-gynecologists and elicited the first, in-depth reactions from the medical profession. There was also support from a group of doctors, lawyers, and other professionals who had formed the Association for the Study of Abortion to bring all sides of the issue to the public. They asked me to join the board. Although they advised me conscientiously, they refused to take a militant political stand.

Only in California did I find a few women dedicated to the overthrow of all prohibitive abortion laws. Patricia Maginnis was thirty-seven when I met her, a slender, almost frail woman with a hesitant, high-pitched voice that disguised the fiery campaigner already making abortion an issue on the West Coast. She had undergone three abortions herself.

She stood on San Francisco street corners handing out lists of Mexican doctors who performed abortions. In 1966, she was arrested under a law banning distribution of lewd and obscene literature. When the trial judge called the law a violation of free speech, Maginnis announced, "Now I can paper the town with leaflets."

As a medical technician in the Women's Army Corps, Maginnis had seen the brutality of the system—"a soldier's wife who had attempted suicide after being refused abortion, held captive like an animal in the hospital ward, literally forced by the staff to continue a pregnancy she hated." Maginnis concluded, "I am ashamed of my country."

Lana Phelan, a pert, handsome blonde who was Maginnis's closest associate, had been pushed into her first marriage at fourteen by family pressure. After one child she was told by her doctor to "stay away from your husband." But Phelan became pregnant again. She located a neighborhood midwife-abortionist. "The pain was indescribable," Phelan remembered, "But at the end this gentle old lady said a few words I'll never forget: 'Did you think it was easy to be a woman?'" Phelan later asked her doctor why he hadn't prescribed contraception, since he had advised her not to have any more children. "I figured you were a smart kid and would find a way out," he told her.[7] At that moment she realized that the whole medical system was rigged against women.

After finishing my book, I saw a few omens indicating my timing had been right. The women's movement had coalesced into the National Organization for Women. I was made a board member since the leadership considered abortion rights crucial to its program. The first inkling that abortion might catch the interest of the public came when the *New York Times Magazine* asked me to do an article, which was published in April 1965. It was the first serious treatment of the religious, philosophic, medical, and social aspects of the subject.

A second break came when *Abortion* was about to be published and *Reader's Digest* carried a condensation of it in May 1966. Lila and DeWitt Wallace had always been devoted to Margaret Sanger and had published parts of my biography of her. Now they brought my radical viewpoint on abortion to a mass audience and sent me on a tour across the country. Many ingredients are required to launch an idea, but timing is paramount. In the case of the abortion rights movement, it was timing that coincided with the demands and aspirations of women that had reached the point of rebellion. The years I had spent agonizing over abortion had provided a fortunate delay. If my book had been published just five years earlier, I have always thought that it would have disappeared from the stores without a ripple.

Still, I was afraid that no one would show up for the opening press conference. I arrived early, cursing Bobbs-Merrill for picking such a cavernous hall on West 57th Street. A few reporters trickled in, then television cameras, soon a flood of them arrived. The hall was jammed. It was obvious the media realized the controversial press potential of abortion. They decided to exploit it.

After a barrage of questions, one reporter asked: "Since you insist women should have the right to abortion, what will you do when a woman asks you for help?" I should have expected a question like that, but I was startled nevertheless. After years of developing a theoretical program, I had suddenly been thrust to the edge of danger. Wasn't it time to make a commitment to action even though it meant the possibility of arrest? In my research I had met a number of doctors performing abortion in the secrecy of their offices, and almost without thinking, I decided to draw on these contacts.

"Yes," I announced. "I want to help women immediately. I'll refer them to skilled doctors. But I also want to test the constitutionality of outdated and punitive laws that must be repealed."

At that point, my life changed completely. Someone had tampered with the system and insisted that no matter how the present laws read, there were constitutional principles that could stop a woman from being forced into an unwanted pregnancy. The conscience of the country must be whipped and goaded. Moral outrage had to be inflamed. An idea had transformed me from a writer into a militant campaigner. An idea I had been mulling over since 1955 would sweep me into a national debate.

NOTES

1. *Baker* v. *Carr,* 369 U. S. 186 (1962).

2. For a study of all state abortion laws before legalization, see Eugene Quay, "Justifiable Abortion—Medical and Legal Foundations," *The Georgetown Law Journal,* v. 49, no. 3, Spring 1961, pp. 395–538.

3. 17 Stat. 598-600 (Forty-Second Congress). Later form of Comstock law appears in 18 *United States Code,* secs. 1471–72 and 19 *United States Code* sec. 1305 (1958).

4. Lawrence Lader, *Abortion,* Bobbs-Merrill, New York, 1966, pp. 79–81, p. 185, fn 9. See Pope Pius IX, *Apostolicae Sedis moderationi.*

5. Finkbine: see Lader, *Abortion,* op. cit., pp. 10–16 from Lader interviews with Sherri and Robert Finkbine. See also fn. p. 178.

6. Lader, *Abortion,* op. cit. p. 173.

7. Maginnis and Phelan quotations from author's interviews for *Abortion II,* Beacon Press, Boston, 1973, pp. 30–34.

4

Desperate Women

What women suffered in the dark years before 1970 is too easily forgotten. Yet their suffering created the movement, brought us together, and drove us forward. It haunted us day and night, made us take risks that no reasonable person would take. Few are around today who helped these women by sending them to capable licensed doctors practicing abortion secretly in their offices. These referrals were the backbone of our early organizing. They confronted the horribly punitive laws. They showed women that something could be done. They were a call to action. The desperation of women, and the referrals that tried to help, must be recorded if we are to understand all the strategies that came later.

From 1965 on, I began receiving phone calls from women pleading for help. Because I was afraid my phone might be tapped, and that some woman callers might be police "plants," I asked women to write me. One frightened woman wrote:

Coming across your article in the January issue of *Look* was an act of fate. In desperation I write to you hoping you can help me as according to your article you have helped so many. . . . Not only do I hate this pregnancy but I fear it also. . . . My emotional state is questionable. I've always considered myself sensible and stable, but in the past 2 months I doubt my sanity. . . . Please help me before I lose my mind. . . . This should be a happy time, but I feel nothing but hate, resentment, pity and despair.

Still another one pleaded:

I am so desperate I am seriously thinking of running my car off the road or shooting myself. . . . I'd rather be dead than pregnant. . . . Please keep this confidential, not even my husband knows I wrote this. But if you can please help me I know he will agree to it because we are both despondent and desperate. Please help me. I *can't* go on any longer.

By return mail I would send each one the phone number of a doctor as near to her home as possible. The doctor in each case would arrange a meeting place and a system of identification aimed at preserving secrecy.

Finding these doctors wasn't easy. A few, like Dr. Robert Spencer in Pennsylvania, had long been a recourse for people I knew. Others, including a fairly prominent author of medical magazine articles, contacted me directly. They had to be checked out, a complex process I tried to accomplish through friends in obstetrics and gynecology. I never had more than seven or eight doctors on my list, and the main problem was that large areas of the country, such as the Southwest, were uncovered.

It must be stressed that the medical profession at the time refused to get involved with those who found themselves with an unwanted pregnancy. State laws punished an abortionist severely, whether licensed doctor or not (in New York, imprisonment for not less than four years or more than twenty years.) But state laws also punished a doctor, or someone like myself, who referred a woman for abortion (in New York, from three months to a year's imprisonment and a fine).[1] "I went to doctor after doctor," wrote a North Carolina woman. "Many listened with tears in their eyes but said they could not help."

"My daughter, eighteen, is in a private psychiatric hospital, following two suicide attempts," wrote an Illinois parent. "Two psychiatrists are recommending a hospital abortion, which meets the legal requirements of the state. However, we have not been able to find either a doctor or a hospital who will handle the case."

I was always dismayed that only a minuscule number of doctors protested the antiquated and inhuman laws, and would take no public stand for their reform. In fact, once the abortion rights movement was organized officially in 1969, it took years to recruit prestigious physicians for our medical committee.

A recurring theme in these early letters, many preserved in my files, was the destruction of family stability as a result of excessive and unwanted childbearing. A twenty-six-year-old New Jersey husband, with a wife of twenty-three, wrote that after her fifth pregnancy, "My wife begged me to let her kill herself. I just held her tight and cried like a baby." A psychiatrist recommended abortion, but the chief surgeon at the hospital insisted that her pregnancy be brought to term even though the mother had to be confined to a mental hospital.

A California husband with four children wrote:

> Today my wife is probably into a mental breakdown. . . .
> She is incapable of doing anything with, or for, the children.
> I am again home from work knowing I can not stay away
> indefinitely without a financial problem. Yet I am afraid to
> leave her.

The physical or mental defects of previous children often drove parents to seek an abortion. A twenty-nine-year-old Ohio mother of six could not get a hospital or doctor to perform an abortion even though her last child was an epileptic. A thirty-nine-year-old Florida mother with three children explained that her last baby "was born abnormal. It lived about three weeks. Then my doctor advised me that it would be dangerous to have any more children." But neither he nor his hospital would help her with an abortion. The plight of older parents was particularly harsh. A Pennsylvania mother, with twelve children and a husband of sixty-nine who was too sick to work, insisted: "If I don't take an overdose of pills, I will lose my sanity."

The saddest irony stemmed from a large group of women who had long used contraception only to have it fail for inexplicable reasons. A New Jersey mother reported:

> After having carefully practiced birth control during nine
> years of marriage, I bitterly resent not having been able to get
> an abortion the one time our methods failed.

A Maryland mother wrote:

We've used the same birth control methods for fourteen years (either a condom or my diaphragm), but something has gone wrong. There's no help in this town as the only gynecologist is a Catholic who won't even recommend birth control pills.

Whereas it was long assumed in that early era that the greatest demand for abortion came from young, single women and those in the lower income and less educated groups, the surprising thing about the letters to me was how many came from media and academic circles. Possibly abortion was being discussed more in liberal and literary journals. But it also can be explained by the fact that accidents and human frailty are universal conditions. One couple I knew lived in a wealthy Connecticut suburb; each had a graduate degree. The wife insisted:

We always used contraception . . . After our fourth child was born mentally defective, we knew it would be stupid to have another baby. Yet we came home late from a Saturday night party, and admittedly, we'd had too much to drink. We tumbled into bed and never thought about birth control. It was one of those human slips that shouldn't have happened.

In 1966, the Clergy Consultation Service on Abortion was organized by ministers and rabbis to advise women on their unwanted pregnancies and often refer them to skilled physicians. One of the ministers was the Rev. Finley Schaef, who invited me to follow a case from the start in order to understand a couple's trauma. We picked the Krales (not their real name). Joe had a modest salary on which he had to support their own child, and one child apiece from each of their previous marriages. His divorce and medical bills forced him to take a second job at night. "When I found out I was pregnant," Mary admitted, "I thought our life was over."

Mary was haunted by the specter of her mother, who had five children, suffered a nervous breakdown and walked out on her father. Eventually she got custody of Mary and her two sisters through the courts, and put them in an orphanage. "I hate my mother for leaving us," Mary said, "but I can see myself doing the same thing if we have any more children."

Mary had even considered going to a back-alley abortionist, one of many hacks who prey on women. These hacks would try to dislodge a fetus with coathangers and other instruments, dangerous chemicals, and rubber tubing. A thirty-four-year-old mother of four, admitted to the emergency room of a city hospital after she had paid a hack abortionist $70 for injection of a soap solution, died seventeen days later. A twenty-nine-year-old mother of three, admitted to an emergency room four days after she had injected herself with a detergent solution, died within nine days.

One Boston city hospital in the pre-legal era admitted an average of six hundred such cases annually; a New York hospital in Harlem about three hundred. One study of seventy-seven cases of "soap intoxication," as doctors called the medical effect of these abortions, revealed forty-three fatalities.[2]

A study in the early 1960s at the University of California's School of Public Health estimated between five thousand and ten thousand abortion deaths annually. Dr. Christopher Tietze placed the figure closer to one thousand, yet about half of all childbearing deaths in New York City were attributed to abortion alone at that time.[3]

Schaef asked whether the Krales would feel any guilt over an abortion. "I don't feel it's a person at this stage," Mary replied. "It's like cells."

Schaef later told me:

> The most astute psychiatrist probably couldn't say for sure, but I think Mary would break down if she were to have another child. I doubt the marriage would survive.

After a few hours' counseling, Schaef gave the Krales the name of a Pennsylvania doctor; two days later, I accompanied them to his office. The doctor told me:

> I only handle a limited number of cases, too few to attract attention. As I interpret the law, all these cases have valid, medical reasons for abortion.

Less than an hour later, Mary came out of the office, smiling happily. The doctor had given her a quick checkup and sedatives, and then a paracervical block to deaden the nerves around the womb. "There wasn't much pain," Mary reported. "The fee was only two hundred dollars. I hugged him when I left." Discussing the case later, Schaef concluded:

> An abortion never solves fundamental problems, yet it can give a couple a chance to rebuild. An unwanted child would have been a disaster for the Krales, and an even worse disaster for the child. "Who knows? A few years from now they may be ready to plan a child to whom they can give the love and care it deserves.

 ⸝ears, after I had referred five hundred women
 ⸜⸜ed doctors, I felt that because no one previously had
access to such a large group of cases, it was time to assess the
reactions of the patients. As a journalism professor at New
York University, I was able to draw on experts in psychology,
sociology, and statistics to create a questionnaire and analyze
the results. The women were instructed not to identify themselves, which, of course, gave them greater freedom in their
responses.[4]

Complete returns came from 282 women. It was hardly an
accurate national sample, but it was the first evidence of the type
of women seeking abortion and their motivations for doing so.
Forty-three percent had family incomes between $5,000 and
$10,000, which must be considered middle class in 1968. Thirty-
two percent had family incomes over $10,000; 23 percent fell
below $5,000. Sixty-seven percent of the respondents had at
least one year of college.

Twenty-eight percent were raised as Catholics (compared to
23 percent nationwide). More recent studies have shown the
same high percentage of Catholics despite the prohibitions of
the church. Fifty-one percent were raised as Protestants; 16
percent as Jews.

Of the 38 percent who were married at the time of the study
(and 10 percent widowed, separated, or divorced), almost all
had at least one child, and most had two children.

Two important figures from the study were that 92 percent
had never had an abortion before, and that 72 percent claimed
they were using contraception at the time of pregnancy. The
first figure can undoubtedly be explained by the difficulty of
securing medical abortion in that era. Most women were forced

into an unwanted pregnancy, with the child either being raised by the mother or another member of the family, or given up for adoption. Contraceptive failure, however, still remains one of the most taxing problems of family planning. Methods can be misused, birth control pills forgotten. Almost all methods have some inherent failure rate. RU 486 has a failure rate of 4 percent. Norplant, which requires the insertion of hormone-releasing rods under the skin, has almost no failures, but it is priced too high for the average family. The only secure method is voluntary sterilization, which depends on the individual's decision to have no more children.

The most portentous results of the study were the affirmative reactions of women. Despite the secrecy involved in the referral process, and the guilt accruing from prohibitive laws and a century of taboos, 55 percent of the respondents reported that their abortions made them "glad without reservation." Two other categories of lesser enthusiasm—"satisfied but doubtful" and "not happy but knew abortion was necessary"—were checked by 8 percent and 33 percent, respectively. Only one respondent said she regretted her abortion.

The women's judgment of their medical care was equally important both to the clergy and other referral services springing up around the country, and to me personally because I had staked my reputation on my selection of doctors. Eighty-two percent of the women concluded that they had suffered no damage from their abortions. Only 11 percent thought there had been emotional damage, a small group that probably persists today even with legal, hospital abortions. "The most competent man I've ever met," one woman rated her doctor. "I have never been so happy and I can't remember feeling healthier," commented another.

Because pain is an important factor in patients' reactions, it was significant that 44 percent of the women who responded stated they had felt little or no pain during the procedure. Twenty-nine percent felt moderate pain and 24 percent labeled abortion painful. Yet even this category usually added such disclaimers as "just a few short pangs—nothing more."

Although most women concluded that abortion had not affected their marriages, a small number were enthusiastic about its impact. "It brought us closer together in many respects," wrote a New Jersey mother. "[It] gave us a more defined goal toward our three sons, brought forth an even greater respect toward each other."

Perhaps the most critical question in the study was whether the woman would ever have another abortion if faced with the possibility again. Seventy-eight percent answered in the affirmative. Five percent were undecided. Only 13 percent said they would never consider it a future option.

The results of this study, when released nationwide in an article in *Look* magazine in early 1969, had a profound effect on advancing the movement. It not only proved the urgency of women's demands to have control of their own bodies and procreative destinies, but also demonstrated that despite the legal prohibitions chaining women, they were determined to overcome all obstacles. And finally, it gave a scientific sanction to the referral services that had become our main strategy in rousing women to organize on a national level. In fact, only a few weeks after the article was published, the National Association for Repeal of Abortion Laws held its founding convention.

For me, the satisfaction came from the wisdom of letters such as one from a pregnant student at a Kansas college. Her father had died leaving her with an ill mother and three younger siblings to support.

> Bringing into the world a child who would be rejected by society, its family, the father and, worst of all, its mother, would be cruel and unfair.

An Ohio mother of four wrote after her abortion: "My emancipation is the joy of my life."

NOTES

All quotations from women's letters in this chapter are taken from letters sent to the author between 1965 and 1973, now in the author's personal possession or in his collection of papers in the manuscript division of the New York Public Library. Names have been erased.

1. *New York Laws* ch. 631, 1, 2, at 1502 (1869); *New York General Statutes,* ch. 181, 1, 2, 3, 4, at 71 (1872).

2. Christopher Tietze, Clyde E. Martin, "Fetal Deaths, Spontaneous and Induced," *Population Studies,* vol. 11, no. 2 (November 1957), pp. 170–76; Ruth Roemer, "Due Process and Organized Health Services," *Public Health Reports* (August 1964); Edwin M. Gold et al., "Therapeutic Abortions in New York City: A Twenty-Year Review," New York Department of Health, Bureau of Records and Statistics (October 14, 1963).

3. For studies on deaths: Lawrence Lader, *Abortion,* Bobbs-Merrill, New York, 1966, pp. 2–3, and p. 176, fn. 1.

4. Lawrence Lader, "First Exclusive Survey of Non-Hospital Abortions," *Look,* January 21, 1969, pp. 63–65.

5

The Big Leap in Abortion Rights

The first year was a lonely time of putting a movement together from tiny building blocks. The Yorkville Democratic club in New York, of which I was an officer, suggested we hold a meeting on abortion, and I invited Assemblyman Percy Sutton of Harlem, who had introduced a moderate reform bill but was swinging towards a more radical position. Other political clubs asked me to speak, followed by churches and synagogues. I came whether we had an audience of ten or a hundred. I took on radio interview shows from stations I had never heard of, and shows by phone from stations in the South where hysterical fundamentalists screamed biblical quotations at me. If only one or two women called me afterwards, there was a chance we could start a local chapter.

Most of my calls came from women seeking abortion. Sometimes they arrived unannounced at my door, and sat weeping on the couch. Letters occasionally enclosed $10 and even $100 bills. I was determined not to make any money from this campaign, and returned every penny, with a friend as witness. On a few occasions, the police called me to inquire about my referrals. I told them to phone my lawyer. Fortunately, I never heard from them again until a Bronx grand jury summoned me in 1969.

Some of the most painful times for me and my wife were the phone calls and letters from cranks. Because I refused to remove my number and address from the telephone book, I was an easy target for fanatics who cursed me on the phone and mailed me pictures of fetuses. They wrote letters with epithets like "murderer" and "beast." When I left or entered my apartment house, I always checked up and down the street to be sure there was no suspicious-looking person who might jump out at me. But gradually this behavior seemed absurd. I gave up my precautions.

One writer, who accused me of making a fortune from referrals, at least had the decency to add his name and address. I wrote him saying I had never made a penny from referrals, but that the cost of postage and stationery and hours lost from my work on articles and books cut into my income. He wrote back calling me a bastard, but enclosing a few dollars worth of stamps.

The flood of appeals for referrals had become so time-consuming and expensive that it was fortunate when three clergymen asked me to lunch in September 1966. They wanted to explore ways to help the movement. The Rev. Howard Moody, a Baptist at Manhattan's Judson Memorial Church; Rev. John Krumm from a nearby Episcopal church; and Rev. Lester Kinsolving, an Episcopal priest from California, were all committed militants. I told them that referrals were the core of our policy of "confrontation politics," which sought to rouse women by challenging the system directly. Even though the referral services kept doctors secret, they announced their mission publicly. I suggested that if the clergy could take on referrals, they would add the dignity and influence of the cloth to the movement.

Rev. Moody promptly began enlisting ministers and rabbis in New York and other cities. Of course, a few interested clergy were forbidden by their congregations to participate. But Rev. Moody stressed the need for community involvement, eventually recruiting hundreds of ministers in twenty states. The New York referral service alone was seeing ten thousand women a year.

The clergy's immediate problem was finding enough good doctors to meet the demand. I turned over my list, including Dr. Edgar Keemer of Detroit and Dr. Robert Spencer of Ashland, Pennsylvania, and the clergy developed further sources of their own. Dr. Spencer's practice treated more children than abortion patients. Trained at the University of Pennsylvania and New York's Rockefeller University, he performed abortions so skillfully that there was only one death in thirty thousand cases (and a jury exonerated him for the death because the patient was already bleeding when she arrived). Dr. Spencer was a folksy, idiosyncratic rebel who kept a statue of Thomas Paine on his desk. Deeply involved in the life of his community, Dr. Spencer belonged to the Rotary Club and was an intimate friend of the mayor, the police chief, and nearly every county official. His abortions had rarely been blocked by law officers because the community valued his services so highly.

Rev. Moody, a six-foot-tall, highly decorated Marine Corps officer in World War II, had built his organization carefully. Yet he was too slow for me. I had hoped for immediate action.

After six months, I decided to prod the clergy in a speech I gave at Cornell University on March 12, 1967. Calling it a "declaration of defiance," the *New York Times* reported that I had already referred three hundred women to the "best medical services," and that a "group of prominent ministers in New York will publicly announce a similar counseling service." The *Times* story said that aiding, abetting, or assisting "illegal abortion" could result in jail terms if the persons were convicted.

Rev. Moody was obviously irked by this premature announcement of his project, but it was my strategy to raise the tempo of action. On May 27, a front-page story in the *Times* announced the opening of the Clergy Consultation Service. Eventually, the Rev. Robert Hare, a Cleveland Presbyterian, was indicted in Massachusetts on a charge of aiding and abetting a criminal abortion. A Cleveland woman, leaving a Chelmsford, Massachusetts, doctor following an abortion, was found by the police to have a notebook listing Rev. Hare's name. The case made headlines throughout the Midwest; the Cleveland *Plain Dealer* insisted that Hare "should not have been in jeopardy of breaking the law by discussing abortion with a woman."

Rev. Hare voluntarily appeared in court in Massachusetts, and his attorney argued that counseling did not constitute aiding and abetting an abortion. The judge dismissed all charges.[1]

At the same time, a court in Oakland, Michigan, issued a warrant for the arrest of Rabbi Max Ticktin, a member of the Chicago Clergy Consultation Service. Chicago police rushed to his office, seizing folders and a telephone. Thomas F. Plunkett, the Oakland prosecutor, gave a lurid description to the press of "An international system of abortion referrals," that he had uncovered. When Plunkett tried to defend his case at a church meeting, he was surrounded by hundreds of angry women, and the Detroit *Free Press,* among other papers, criticized Michigan's punitive abortion law. Shortly thereafter Plunkett announced that he would not seek to extradite Ticktin from Chicago to Michigan.[2]

The consultation service became an enormous asset to the abortion rights movement. By June 1970, the number of cases processed in New York had reached thirty thousand. Los Angeles was referring a thousand women a month.

My Cornell speech produced further strategic results. I was an officer of the Association for the Study of Abortion (ASA), a group of prominent doctors and lawyers who, unfortunately, refused to take a militant stand. The *New York Times* telephoned Dr. Robert E. Hall, its president. According to the article, he "disassociated both himself and the group from Mr. Lader's action" on referrals. This marked a turning point, separating the moderates from activists like myself and Ruth Smith, who had been recently forced to resign as ASA's executive director. We promptly banded together to organize for complete repeal of punitive abortion laws.

Miraculously, neither Rev. Moody nor I were harassed by detectives or district attorneys for the next year or so. Then, on May 23, 1969, the administrator for the Bronx doctors, to whom I had referred hundreds of women, telephoned to tell me he had just been jailed. I quickly provided him with a lawyer, who reported, "The assistant district attorney mentioned your name a few times. You'll certainly be hearing from him."

At least a thousand letters from women asking for help were stored in my closet. Stupidly, and because precious time did not permit it, I had failed to black out their names or addresses. Now I worried that detectives might be on my doorstep in a few minutes to seize the records that would implicate these women in court. Frantically I stuffed every letter into two, huge suitcases, and dashed a few blocks away to a friend who had a large fireplace. We burned all of them, a defensive move that unfortunately destroyed the sociological evidence of the roots of abortion rights.

The Bronx district attorney, Burton Roberts, was noted for his flair for publicity. A magazine headline called him the "Toughest District Attorney in New York." He obviously enjoyed describing the doctors' group to the press as an "abortion mill" in a "plush and luxurious" apartment-clinic. "Many of the referrals were made by clergymen," he claimed. The *Daily News* gave the story front-page headlines: "NAB 4 IN BRONX ABORTION MILL."[3]

The possibility of arrest had always existed, but I had refused to think about it. Now my immunity had suddenly collapsed. I had become a target. The specter of police, the district attorney, and a court proceeding were a frightening probability that I could not shake off. I was subpoenaed to appear before a grand jury.

When I faced the Bronx grand jury with Rev. Moody, Rev. Jesse Lyons of the Riverside Church, and Rev. Finley Schaef of the Washington Square Methodist Church, my numbness was replaced by a sense of exaltation. When I went into the court room, I felt that success hinged on my performance. The jury of twenty-three men and women sat on rising tiers of seats— like a theater. I stood before them on a small platform.

My lawyer had instructed me to take the Fifth Amendment

and to answer only yes or no to every question, without any elaboration. Instead, after an assistant district attorney showed my book and articles to the jury and asked why I had begun making doctor referrals, I decided to use this opportunity to state the movement's position. I explained exactly how we had progressed from reform laws to favorable judicial decisions, and that at this moment many New York State legislators were proposing a bill that would make this hearing pointless. When the district attorney asked me how much money I made from referrals, I said I had made nothing. I returned every dollar sent me with witnesses to prove it.

I left the grand jury room with growing excitement. They had listened carefully, and perhaps grasped the absurdity of the Bronx raid in the context of the abortion rights campaign.

When the grand jury announced its indictments, no charges were brought against the clergy or myself, only against doctors and nurses arrested in the raid. They were eventually released with the payment of fines. It was a boost for referral services. Even District Attorney Roberts would brazenly claim: "I was the first D.A. in the city to say that the old abortion law was not serving the community."[4]

In 1966 and 1967, I tried to help people like State Representative (later governor) Richard Lamm and Ruth Steel of Colorado pass the first American Law Institute legislation. The ALI model was a small step forward, but at least the process brought debate. It allowed abortion for rape, incest, and occasionally "health" when approved by a hospital medical committee. If it fell short of total rights, I wanted it to make the public realize the need for change. What I sought was a strategy that went to the very core of the problem. In 1966, I met regu-

larly with a group to work out a test case that could be brought
to federal court, based on the precedent established in the
Supreme Court's *Griswold* v. *Connecticut* decision of 1965.

We sought a respected obstetrician-gynecologist who would
use the pattern of a case in Britain. The doctor would openly
perform an abortion in his hospital on a patient with a minor
health problem—a case that clearly contravened the laws of
New York. We would subsequently notify the district attorney.
If the doctor was arrested and tried, we would attempt to have
the case carried to the U. S. Supreme Court to affirm a constitutional basis for abortion.

The people attempting to put this case together were friends
of mine. Dr. William Ober, a pathologist, and Cyril Means, a
lawyer, were at Harvard University in my day. Aryeh Neier was
with the New York Civil Liberties Union, one of the first organizations to back abortion rights. Ephraim London, a lawyer,
had been one of my closest advisers from the start. Harriet
Pilpel was not only Margaret Sanger's lawyer but also the
lawyer for the Planned Parenthood Federation of America. I
drew on close contacts for each important project. These dedicated professionals were not only trustworthy but in a struggle
where many could "burn out" quickly, these friends had great
staying power.

Theoretically, our blueprint for a constitutional case seemed
sound. Our problem was finding a doctor willing to take the
risks of possible malpractice and criminal charges. Even in
1969, when a national movement was organized, the medical
profession was fearful of taking any stand that would threaten
profits. Hospitals were worse. Locked into boards and bureau-
cracies, they worried ceaselessly about offending donors, or

amending administrative rules. So our test case disappeared. Yet symbolically, it was the precursor of *Roe* v. *Wade*, which legalized abortion seven years later.

I was still seeking a test case when I finally found it in 1968 through Dr. Milan Vuitch of Washington, D.C., to whom I had sent many referrals. As I studied state laws on abortion, I discovered that the District of Columbia permitted abortion for *health* reasons, unlike almost all other state statutes, in which abortion was permissible only to save the *life* of the mother. "Life" was obviously an impossible test to meet. Because the World Health Organization defined health as a complete state of both mental and physical well-being, not just the absence of disease and infirmity, it occurred to me that this gave us a broad basis for testing the law. I urged Dr. Vuitch to make detailed records on the condition of every patient.[5]

Dr. Vuitch was ideal for a test case. He was pugnacious and brash. Born in Serbia in 1915, he graduated from medical school in Budapest, Hungary, and later interned at Doctors Hospital in the District of Columbia. Dr. Vuitch was certified by the American Board of Surgery. "I'm breaking the way," he liked to say. "I'm getting rid of medical absurdities." Another advantage to having Dr. Vuitch involved in the test case was the fact that he practiced abortion openly, mixing abortion patients with his regular practice. He instructed me to give his name and phone number openly to women seeking abortions.

On May 1, 1968, police burst into his office at the very moment that an abortion patient was on the table.

This woman had described her mental suffering—her husband's frequent desertions and his extramarital affairs. She had an unwanted pregnancy by a husband she detested. It was all down on my chart . . . Only I, as her doctor, can decide if her health has been threatened. Can the police, can some district attorney make this decision? Of course not.

Following our strategy, Dr. Vuitch's lawyers, Joseph Nellis and Joseph Sitnick, delivered a frontal assault on the constitutionality of the law of the District of Columbia. They held that the rights of both the doctor and the patient had been abridged under the First, Fourth, Fifth, and Ninth Amendments to the U.S. Constitution. A woman's sovereignty over her own body must be guaranteed in accordance with the 1965 *Griswold* v. *Connecticut* decision of the U.S. Supreme Court. The District of Columbia statute was unconstitutional because it failed to meet the specificity requirements in the due process clause of the Fifth Amendment.

On November 10, 1969, in the first federal court decision to overthrow an anti-abortion law, Judge Arnold Gesell declared that the Washington, D.C., law gave "no clear standard to guide the doctor, the jury or the Court," and ruled that previous Supreme Court decisions provided a right of privacy in "family, marriage and sex matters." The immediate impact of Judge Gesell's decision was to allow any physician in Washington, D.C., to perform an abortion according to his medical judgment. It also unleashed a flood of other test cases in federal and state courts around the country.[6]

In those early years, I often tried to understand why I had been swept into organizing a social movement. I realized that I loved the challenge. I felt immense satisfaction by making an idea work, and proving that my strategies were bringing results.

A vital objective of abortion advocates was to draw major groups into the movement. The fledgling women's groups were a basic ingredient. I had known Betty Friedan since the days in New York in 1941 when she roomed with some of my Vassar friends. I had seen her almost daily in the Frederic Lewis Allen Room for writers at the New York Public Library. At that time, she was working on her significant book, *The Feminine Mystique.* When she put together the National Organization for Women in 1966, its members ignored abortion at first. At NOW's national convention in 1967, young militants from all over the country demanded an abortion rights plank. Friedan was able to get it passed, but a number of conservative delegates resigned.

The turning point came at the Washington Square Methodist Church in New York City when hundreds of women, organized by "Red Stockings," the most radical feminist group, stood up to describe their abortions, their anguished search for help, the dingy rooms of hack practitioners, and the degradation that stained their lives for years. For the first time women had made the public understand their personal horror.

Mass anger was essential to our campaign. The first violent confrontation—"WOMEN BREAK UP ABORTION HEARING," as the *New York Times* described it—came at a state legislative hearing in New York City on February 13, 1969. The panel was all male. Of fifteen witnesses, all were men except one Catholic nun. At the start, a woman in the audience shouted: "Now let's hear from real experts— the women!" State Senator Norman Lent kept pounding his gavel, but another woman broke in: "Men don't get pregnant. They just make the laws." The shouting continued until Lent moved the panel to another room, posted policemen outside the door, and refused to allow the public inside. Hundreds of women sat down outside the door for hours until Lent finally allowed three of their representatives to speak.[7]

In the first year of the abortion rights movement, the only religious group to join us as an official body was the Unitarian-Universalists. With other faiths, I was required to work behind the scenes through personal contacts such as Rev. Rodney Shaw of the Methodists and Rev. Krumm of the Episcopalians. Physicians Forum, a liberal doctors' group, followed by the large and influential American Public Health Association, quickly supported us. The American Civil Liberties Union was an early ally.

The Planned Parenthood Federation of America had to be won over both for its status and its power. I hoped to employ my long friendship with Margaret Sanger for this objective but, unfortunately, she was already seriously ill and unable to discuss the proposal. She died in the fall of 1966. Planned Parenthood during that period continued to be dominated by suburban matrons who wanted no part of abortion. One center of influence was Dr. Alan Guttmacher, who would shortly become the federation president. I knew him well, but I also knew that he adopted a careful line. When the National Association for Repeal of Abortion Laws (NARAL) was founded in Chicago in February 1969, I had trouble convincing Dr. Guttmacher to speak at the plenary session. I had to play all my cards, something I rarely did. I told Alan he owed me a personal favor for my work on the Margaret Sanger biography, with its value to family planning.

Alan finally came to Chicago, where he was heckled by radicals in the audience. Yet I never regretted having put pressure on him. He slowly moved towards the repeal position. A few years later, he was a key figure in bringing Planned Parenthood into the abortion movement.

A sensitive issue was whether we would first proceed with American Law Institute legislation. There was no early group consensus because the abortion rights movement remained chaotic and spontaneous. Yet I have always believed that our great strength came from the local level. Every group had its own boiling energy. There was no control by a central authority. When I flew to Chicago to make a speech in October 1966, I had breakfast with Dr. Lonny Myers, a bright, rambunctious leader of the Illinois Committee for the Medical Control of Abortion. She was opposed, as I was, to stopgap ALI legislation. Dr. Myers soon recruited ten thousand members, resulting in the strongest chapter in the country.

Even a spineless ALI law moved the campaign forward. In California, Assemblyman Anthony Beilenson was instrumental in putting through an ALI law in 1967. As a congressman, Beilenson became one of the strongest advocates of the repeal position. Ironically, the California bill was signed in 1967 by Gov. Ronald Reagan, who as president led a virulent attack on abortion rights.

In New York State, we were building a strong base among legislators and political clubs. One surprise supporter was State Senator Basil Paterson, a black Catholic from Harlem, who told the legislature:

We're not telling other Catholics they have to get abortions. We're only asking them not to dictate to the rest of the population what they can and cannot do.

The smart strategy in New York was to oppose the ALI bill, introduced by Assemblyman Albert Blumenthal. It failed to pass in 1968, but almost got through in 1969, until a Nassau County legislator quixotically switched his vote. When our local chapter sent a flood of letters to his office, he reversed his position once again. The mood appeared ready for repeal. I discussed the possibility for an all-out bill with Manhattan Borough President Percy Sutton, Assemblyman Franz Leichter, a Manhattan Democrat, and Assemblywoman Constance Cook, an upstate Republican.

A strategic quandary was whether we should back legislation, or rely on crucial judicial cases. I urged the movement to keep a balance between the two. The Vuitch case had been planned, but others appeared almost accidentally. In 1967 in Los Angeles, Dr. Leon Belous, a noted obstetrician-gynecologist at Cedars of Lebanon Hospital, gave a married woman the telephone number of a qualified California doctor who performed abortions. The police, probably tipped off by another patient, raided the doctor's office, found Dr. Belous's name in his record books, and arrested Dr. Belous. "I decided to make a stand on constitutional grounds because I knew I was right," Belous insisted. In September 1969, the California Supreme Court in a four-to-three decision ruled the former state law unconstitutional and exonerated Belous. In a crucial opinion, which undoubtedly influenced *Roe* v. *Wade* four years later, the California court declared:

> The fundamental right of a woman to choose whether to bear children follows from the Supreme Court's and this court's repeated acknowledgment of a "right of privacy" or "liberty" in matters related to marriage, family and sex.

California hospitals and clinics would soon perform 135,000 legal abortions a year.[8]

Ruth Smith and I were planning a press conference in the fall of 1968 for the introduction of the Cook-Leichter repeal bill in the New York legislature when Dr. Lonny Myers of Chicago met us at my apartment on July 30. It turned out to be a portentous meeting. Lonny wanted to stage the "First National Conference on Abortion Laws" in Chicago during the following winter. She proposed bringing together every political, feminist, medical, and religious group whose members wanted a change in the abortion laws. We all agreed that a radical groundswell had reached nationwide proportions. I had two concerns. Having been involved in conferences before, I knew the huge amount of organizational work required. I declined to participate unless the last day of the conference would be devoted to forming a national organization that would make our efforts worthwhile.

I insisted that the national organization have a repeal position—let the moderates walk out if they didn't like it. Ruth and Lonny agreed to this demand.

The dates were set for February 14–16, 1969. We formed a coordinating committee of Prof. Garrett Hardin on the West Coast, Lonny in the Midwest, myself in the East. None of us realized that six months of torturous organizing lay ahead.

I was now taking a step that would propel me into national leadership and completely consume my career. I suppose I was motivated by the fact that the radicalism I had learned from Congressman Vito Marcantonio was crushed by McCarthyism. As a result of the Cold War, the country had sunk into an apathy that was only now being challenged by the Black movement, the women's movement, and Lyndon Johnson's social legislation (the War on Poverty). I believed that a national abortion rights movement would bring fresh purpose to people's lives.

We concentrated on influential names for our honorary officers, drawing on personal contacts: Congresswoman Shirley Chisholm, the first black woman in the House of Representatives, whom I knew from New York politics; U.S. Senator Maurine Neuberger of Oregon, who had replaced her late husband, Dick Neuberger, a friend of mine in the magazine business. It was remarkable even in late 1968 how few major groups agreed to be associated with abortion rights. Although Lonny mailed invitations to everyone with even the slightest interest in the subject, I focused on people whom I knew were dedicated to repeal. When the critical debate occurred in Chicago, I needed as many allies as possible.

Month after month we were on the phone with each other two or three times a day. Lonny wrote me:

> It is now 3 A.M., another night without sleep. When my eight-year-old asked me to play something last night, it was all I could do not to have a tantrum. Then she patted me on the head and said, "There, there, mother, it's all right."

Just one major organization, the American Public Health Association, permitted its president to make a keynote speech. Dr. Guttmacher, of course, would speak for himself, not for Planned Parenthood. We had to rely on veteran hardliners such as Betty Friedan, Manhattan Borough President Percy Sutton, and the Rev. Howard Moody of the Clergy Consultation Service. Enough money had to be scraped together because no foundation took us seriously. A few wealthy people like Hugh Moore, former president of the Dixie Cup company, Beatrice McClintock, and her sister, Dr. Helen Edey, provided early funding.

It seems almost unbelievable today, when the budget for the National Abortion Rights Action League runs into millions of dollars, that the conference was put together on $3,500, with $6,000 set aside for creating the new National Association for Repeal of Abortion Laws.

NARAL's First National Conference convened at the Drake Hotel in Chicago on February 14, 1969. Large delegations came from California, the Midwest, New York, Pennsylvania, and the East Coast. There were 350 delegates representing fifty organizations. Most of us had never met before, and I stayed up late at night talking with people who had previously been just voices on the phone.

Luncheon and dinner speakers set long-range goals, but the core of the conference consisted of workshops on legislative and judicial action, public education, and referral services. The central debate came over a plank supporting an outright repeal of the old abortion laws and free referral services. I had pushed for this plank and lobbied hard for it, convinced that a decision had to be made quickly and cleanly if the momentum of the conference was not to be lost.

For hours, speaker after speaker took the microphone to argue their positions. Moderates feared the country wasn't ready for repeal, that rash action would lose potential supporters, and that referral services might involve us in endless lawsuits. The auditorium often overflowed with both tension and anger. Big delegations from California, Illinois, and New York, with Maginnis, Myers, and myself as spokespersons, argued that only repeal could rouse the country. Anything less could bring lethargy and retreat. In the final vote, we won at least two-thirds of the delegates.

I did not expect the turmoil of the last day when I chaired a session to establish the National Association for Repeal of Abortion Laws. I had sat up most of the night with state and local caucuses, believing we could draw up an organizational structure that satisfied the majority. Debate flared up immediately. Each delegate voiced individual opinions on the direction NARAL should take.

As the afternoon dragged on, I despaired that we would never reach a consensus. It was obviously an illusion to believe that hundreds of philosophies and temperaments would agree on a structure in a few hours. With delegates leaving for trains and planes, someone finally suggested a compromise. The whole problem should be decided by a "steering committee" of twelve with the authority to draw up a constitution and nominate a board of directors who would eventually be approved by a mail-in vote of all delegates. The committee, some from the Midwest and the West, but mainly from the East, included Friedan, Lonny Myers, Sutton, Stewart Mott, and me.

That night I boarded a plane for New York, angry, frustrated, and depressed. I felt we had lost the opportunity to make NARAL a viable organization. I feared the steering committee would die of inertia. I was so pessimistic that I left for a brief vacation and missed the first meeting. When I returned, I was told that I had been elected chairman. Actually, the committee turned out to be both energetic and forceful. We hired a salaried executive director, Lee Gidding, a woman experienced in feminist issues. We rented a tiny office on West 57th Street. Then we set out to nominate a board of almost one hundred people representing every area of the country.

On May 8, 1969, coinciding with Mother's Day, we organized "Days of Anger" in Atlanta, Los Angeles, Philadelphia, and many other cities. In front of the Trenton, New Jersey, State House, mothers wheeled their baby carriages, handed out soft drinks and cookies, and carried signs proclaiming, "Illegal Abortions Support the Mafia." In New Haven, Connecticut, a Catholic priest joined a picket line around a hospital, protesting the hypocrisy of the medical profession. Manhattan Borough President Sutton led two hundred picketers around Lenox Hill Hospital in New York.[9]

After the delegates approved the new board by mail, its members met in New York on September 17 and elected New York City Councilwoman Carol Greitzer as president. I was the chairman of the executive committee. Few of us, including the media, realized that this was a historic moment. The *New York Times* did not report the founding conference in Chicago until many days later. When NARAL was looking for a picture of the Chicago event for the celebration of the twentieth anniversary, we canvassed every delegate we could reach and searched newspaper files but did not find a single photograph.[10] I now realize that not one press photographer or TV camera had been present. The coordinators did not hire a cameraman. We were so consumed with the job of making history, we had neglected to record it.

NOTES

1. Cleveland *Press,* June 24, 1969; Cleveland *Plain Dealer,* June 12, 1969 p.1; March 29, 1970; National Council of Churches *Bulletin*, May 4, 1970, pp. 12–15; Boston *Herald Traveller*, June 11, 1969, p. 6.

2. Chicago *Sun-Times,* January 8–11, 1970; Chicago *Daily News,* January 7, 1970, p. 1; Detroit *Free Press,* January 5, 1970, p. D1; January 13, 20, 1970.

3. *New York Times*, October 17, 1969, p. 28; New York *Daily News,* October 17, 1969, p. 1.

4. Author's interview with Roberts, October 16, 1969.

5. For Dr. Vuitch: Lawrence Lader, *Abortion II,* Beacon Press, Boston, 1973, pp. 1–14.

6. *United States* v. *Vuitch,* 305 F. Supp. 1032 (D.D.C. 1969), jurisdiction postponed to argument on merits 397 U.S. 1061 (1970)

7. *New York Times,* February 14, 1969, p. 42; *New Yorker,* February 22, 1969, p. 28.

8. *People* v. *Belous,* 71 Cal. 2d 954, 458 P 2d 194, 80 Cal. Rptr. p. 354 (1969), cert. denied, 397 U.S. 915 (1970).

9. Philadelphia *Tribune,* 9 May 1969; Newark *Evening News,* May 9, 1969.

10. *New York Times,* February 17, 1969

6

Impossible Victories:
Abortion Rights (1969–1973)

From our tiny office on West 57th Street, with one staff director and a secretary, the National Association for Repeal of
Abortion Laws (NARAL) set out to convert the country virtually overnight. Our initial plan was to concentrate on states
that had the best chance of passing repeal laws, particularly
California, Illinois, New York, and Washington. The opposition
was hardening. Whenever we debated them on television, they
held up to the camera gigantic, blown-up photographs of what
they said were ten-week-old fetuses, "almost human persons,"
but they were actually fetuses of fourteen or more weeks of gestation. It was brutal, bound to disturb the viewing audience. We
realized we had to fight such exaggerations quickly, even if it
meant using the same crude tactics as our opponents.

We secured authenticated pictures from a Midwest sheriff's office of women lying on the floors of dingy motel rooms
after botched abortions. They had bled to death after punctur-
ing their wombs with catheters and other frightful, self-abortion
techniques—the terror forced on women by unjust laws. We
brought these enlarged pictures to all our television debates,

demanding the same right as the opposition to use theirs. The audience protest was so strong that broadcasters decided to ban all displays.

In our determination to overthrow the old laws and save women's lives, we often took risks whose outcomes were far from certain. In Michigan in 1971, our state affiliate wanted to risk an initiative and referendum, which meant going directly to voters on legalized abortion. The NARAL board doubted we had enough strength, but our Michigan group gathered 305,000 petition signatures. Polls indicated we were backed by 60 percent of the electorate.

Our shortage of money was critical in Michigan and almost everywhere else. We had only a few big donors in that period. Our foremost angel was Joe Sunnen, a St. Louis inventor, who, as a sideline, had developed a spermicidal jell. Crusty and irrepressible, Sunnen would meet us at a restaurant and roam from table to table, passing out samples of his jell to diners and waitresses alike. Another large donor was a shy, aristocratic woman from the East Coast. I flew to her city and presented our case to her staff (she never appeared in person), and she gave us $30,000, the biggest gift we had so far received. Unfortunately, it wasn't enough money to win in Michigan. Just before the referendum, the Catholic opposition poured some $300,000 into a broadcast and a print campaign. When the referendum came to a vote in 1972, we lost by 40 to 60 percent.

The opposition represented a strange brand of fanaticism. I always believed that anyone who thought that a fetus was a human person from the moment of conception had a right to that opinion. It was their right to educate and possibly change others through religious groups, speeches, or street-corner meetings. That was the pluralistic American tradition. Yet these fanatics wanted to return society to the religious tyranny of bygone Europe when only one set of beliefs was tolerated. They were determined to convert everyone. This was a crusade to use both the law and legislatures to stamp their system on the nation.

It was difficult to grasp the roots of this fanaticism, which began, of course, with the religious conviction that the meeting of sperm and egg immediately produces a human person. I personally believe it goes deeper than that. It appears to stem from a hatred of women, and the need to keep women subservient to their husbands, blocking them from careers, education, and self-expression. The apparent goal was to solidify male power and to punish women who experienced unwanted pregnancies.

The anti-abortionists have another motive: promoting a political agenda. They use the abortion issue as the cutting edge for right-wing issues such as opposing gun control. Although they represent only 15 percent of the population, according to our measurements, they want political domination and seek to control the Republican party.

Polls show that Catholics, despite the proclamations of their bishops, use abortion as regularly as any other religious group. From the beginning, NARAL's policy was to appeal to Catholic moderates. When a courageous group, including a contingent of nuns, organized Catholics for a Free Choice in 1973, NARAL supplied the seed money. It was one of the wisest decisions we ever made.[1]

NARAL's strategy was hammered out at executive committee meetings. As chair, I favored unity, but it soon became apparent we had split into two factions. The majority, which included Betty Friedan, Cyril Means, Lana Phelan, and myself, demanded unrelenting militancy. Others, whom I dubbed the "go-slowers," represented money and status. We clashed over abortion referral networks. We militants believed in political confrontation no matter what the risks.

In this we followed history. Before the Civil War, the abolitionists forced the country to confront the horrors of slavery by hiding escaped slaves. These reformers risked arrest by removing slaves from northern jails. Abolitionist leader William Lloyd Garrison said, "Tell a man whose house is on fire to give a moderate alarm."[2] I followed the lessons of Margaret Sanger, who had frequently been jailed for opening her Brooklyn clinic and breaking other anticontraception laws. Most of us in NARAL thought the house was on fire, and we knew extreme measures were needed.

When Rev. Howard Moody, other clergy, and I were called before the Bronx grand jury in 1969, my faction of NARAL submitted a motion that referral services should be backed in public statements, and legal costs be paid in case of trial. The minority opposed us. Fortunately, no one was indicted, but we won in the executive committee by only a few votes. The unity of NARAL had been strained.

Principles rather than personalities brought about these disagreements. We now were convinced that any commercial taint had to be removed from NARAL. No officer or board member in that early period received a salary, but the opposition frequently charged us with profiting from abortion referrals and kickbacks, an allegation that was totally false. Roy Lucas, chair of our legal committee, however, received fees to represent a few doctors who were performing abortions and who had not only run afoul of the police but had charged women excessively in our view. The executive committee told him that his involvement could damage NARAL. We asked him to give up such cases but he refused. We then asked him to resign from the board, and he refused again.

The crisis became so acute that the matter was taken to the membership. The debate turned nasty. Although the majority had the votes and Lucas was forced to resign, I was disturbed by the internal split within NARAL. Perhaps we were too rigid, but NARAL had to be built on inflexible moral principles. The Roy Lucas case remains puzzling. He was a fine conversationalist and delightful company. My wife and I often invited him and his wife to dinner, but they were soon divorced. His ex-wife went on to gain a Ph.D. and, ironically, rose to an influential position in the abortion rights movement, a position that Lucas should have held. Lucas was a brilliant lawyer and at first had a notable record. Yet his aggressiveness often resulted in personal confrontations, particularly with Sarah Weddington's handling of *Roe* v. *Wade*. Consequently Lucas gave up the law and turned to carpentry and painting. He dropped out of sight and lived a day-to-day existence, principally in the Rocky Mountain area; a peculiar life after a once-golden career that could have brought him to the forefront of the abortion rights movement.

All our conflicts were carefully kept from the public, but at one national convention Bill Baird, a board member from Long Island, New York, turned his animosity into a public relations spectacle. He had long feuded with Betty Friedan, another board member, because she had once charged him with being a male chauvinist. Instead of bringing a complaint to the board, as I begged him to do, Baird increased his attacks on Friedan with large poster boards carried by a few of his followers. They paraded up and down in front of the hotel where we were meeting. Consequently, the media never covered the important issues at the convention, but seized on this picketline and gave it top billing on the front pages and the television news.

Baird was an enigma. I admired his work, including an early abortion clinic, and got him on the NARAL board until other members became so exasperated with him that he was forced out. Flamboyant and aggressive, Baird never gave the opposition a moment's peace. In May 1965, he dispensed contraceptives from his van in Hempstead, New York. After he demanded that the police arrest him he spent the night in jail. He turned his attention to abortion in 1967. Inviting the press and the police to his Hempstead clinic, he read off the names of a few doctors providing abortion in Mexico and Japan, yet became furious when officers refused to arrest him.

Although Baird's jailings had satisfied his hunger for martyrdom, he had made an outstanding contribution in the case of *Eisenstadt* v. *Baird.* On April 6, 1967, he addressed a student audience at Boston University, making sure that both police and an ACLU lawyer were present. When he offered to distribute packages of contraceptive foam (sold at many Massachusetts drug stores without prescription), twelve unmarried girls accepted the packages. The police then arrested him.

A Massachusetts law, labeled "Crimes Against Chastity," forbade the distribution of contraceptives to unmarried persons. The assistant district attorney called Baird's speech "an invitation to promiscuity and sexual license." Baird was found guilty and later sentenced to three months in jail. But after a storm of public protest the governor pardoned him and he won release from jail in a month.

The U.S. Court of Appeals for the First Circuit soon declared the chastity law unconstitutional. In March 1972, the U.S. Supreme Court corroborated its unconstitutionality in a six-to-one vote. Justice William J. Brennan's opinion ruled:

If the right of privacy means anything, it is the right of the individual, married or single, to be free from unwarranted intrusion into matters so fundamentally affecting a person as the decision whether to bear or beget a child.[3]

Despite the impact of this case, Baird constantly infuriated almost everyone in the abortion movement. He staged a sitdown in front of Planned Parenthood in New York City, labeling it a wasteful, hidebound bureaucracy. He constantly attacked women's groups for banning him from their meetings. He often complained to the press that no one had given him proper recognition. He became a pariah to the feminists, an isolated figure who diminished what could have been a distinguished career.

In the early days, NARAL sought the fastest route to legalized abortion. The courts offered a convenient approach since the burden fell on our lawyers and cooperating groups like the ACLU. The legislative approach, by contrast, demanded intense organizing and huge amounts of money. After our success in federal court in the Vuitch case, permitting abortion on "health" grounds, we discovered it had been only a paper breakthrough. Washington's three voluntary hospitals, particularly D.C. General, ignored the court and rejected most applicants. We believed the time had come for confrontation. With help from the ACLU, we went to the U.S. Court of Appeals in 1970, which ordered that a woman whose emotional health might be damaged by carrying a fetus to term be accepted after certification by one or two psychiatrists. Yet there was only a trickle of patients. We had to go back to court again before D.C. General finally agreed to accept a thousand mental health cases a year.

We then concentrated on legislation. With the broadest coalition yet assembled, ranging from the U.S. Chamber of Commerce to the AFL-CIO, we pushed through a repeal bill in Hawaii in early 1970. When the legislature passed a repeal bill in Alaska only to have it vetoed by the governor, the veto was overridden by one vote, coming from a Catholic woman senator.

In late 1969, we decided to take the ultimate gamble by pouring our resources into a New York bill. It was a critical state, yet the obstacles were formidable. There were 6.5 million Catholics (about 40 percent of the population), and a heavy concentration of Republicans upstate. Moreover, the archdiocese, located on 50th Street in Manhattan, had long been known as the "powerhouse," and wielded great influence over the New York state legislature. It was a political rule that no bill could be passed without the cardinal's blessing.

On the positive side, we had built a strong network of Democratic and a few Republican clubs. Our coalition of religious groups was larger than in any other state. Catholics such as Basil Paterson in the Senate and Charles Rangel in the Assembly were key sponsors of the bill. The prime mover was Constance Cook, an astute upstate Republican who was close to Gov. Nelson Rockefeller. The governor told her he would sign the bill if it was passed. By an accident of legislative history, we had another political advantage. Cardinal Francis Spellman was concentrating in this session on repeal of the "Blaine amendment" to the state constitution, which barred public funding of religious schools. Catholic insiders informed us that some Catholic legislators might agree to vote for the abortion bill as long as legislative weight was put behind repeal of the Blaine amendment.

NARAL and its state affiliate worked closely with Cook lining up votes. By January 1970, we were close to a majority in both houses. At this point, we reached a disturbing impasse. The bill never required that abortions be performed by a licensed physician. This was a purposeful strategy. We had always taken the position that paramedicals (nurses and medical technicians trained in the procedure) could perform abortion as well as any doctor. Their inclusion might become essential if hospitals and their doctors were laggard about setting up abortion services.

Cook's vote count, however, proved we could never win a majority in both houses unless the bill stipulated that only licensed physicians could perform abortions. This provoked a crisis. Our New York affiliate refused to yield on paramedicals. Weighing political reality and the chance to pass a bill of immeasurable significance against our personal convictions, the NARAL executive committee voted to accept the doctor-only limitation. I voted with the majority. It seemed urgent at the time, but in the long run we may regret this compromise. With the erosion of legal abortion in the 1990s, the survival of medical facilities in many states could eventually shift from doctors, increasingly pressured to resign after extremist harassment, to trained paramedicals recruited primarily for their courage, and already used in a few clinics.

In late February, our campaign was frustrated by an unexpected move. Sen. Earl Brydges, a Catholic and the majority leader, took the initiative away from Cook by submitting his own bill. Amazingly, it removed all restrictions on abortion, even removing it from the criminal code. Our strategists considered it a hoax, a bill so radical that the Senate would have to reject it. Yet Brydges may have underestimated the rising support for abortion rights, and the bill passed by a vote of thirty-one to twenty-six. Startled, Brydges announced the next day that he would fight for strict limitations on his own bill.

Suddenly the Catholic church grasped the seriousness of the challenge. At Easter Sunday services, every bishop and priest in the state read a blistering denunciation of the bill, which allowed abortion through twenty-four weeks of pregnancy (the accepted point of viability) in the conformed Senate and Assembly versions. Catholic legislators known to support the bill were branded "murderers." Priests and nuns roamed the floor of the legislature, lobbying openly. A few Catholics buckled under the pressure and switched their positions.

The mood of the repeal forces was grim; we soon lost two votes we had counted on. We had to gain Arthur Eve of Buffalo and Mary Anne Krupsak of Amsterdam-Schenectady to balance our losses Eve was black, and Barbara Gelobter, a black feminist and friend of mine from Manhattan, was working on him. Krupsak came from a devout Catholic family, and her father's pharmacy was continuously picketed by anti-abortionists. Even if we won both votes, we could only have a tie. Our ultimate concentration had to be on Hulan Jack, a black from New York's Harlem.

On the morning of April 9th, Gelobter and I were searching desperately for black leaders to pressure Jack. I kept calling Manhattan Borough President Percy Sutton in New York, but he was rushing to Albany and was soon closeted with Jack. We kept phoning other blacks for help as if the act of dialing the telephone could relieve our panic.

The floor of the Assembly began to fill. The opposition presented one diluting amendment after another, which we beat down. "Murderers," screamed a woman from the galleries. The bill "will permit a mother to kill her child for whatever reason strikes her fancy," a Suffolk Republican announced on the floor. At 4:30 P.M., Cook called for a vote, and there was a sudden hush. The moment had come after five years of campaigning. Once we would have been lucky to draw sixty listeners at a political club. Now the legislators of the second largest state in the United States were on the verge of revolutionizing our political and social system. The slow roll call began. We lost the two votes we had worried about, but we gained the votes of Eve and Krupsak, amidst bursts of applause. Then Jack, the swing vote, voted no. There was anguish among our workers, who were gathered at the rim of the floor. The vote would end in a tie, seventy-four to seventy-four, unless we could pick up one vote switch in the fading moments.

Just seconds before the clerk would announce the tally, George Michaels, a Democrat from Auburn, rose to his feet. His face was contorted, his eyes filled with tears. In fragmented sentences, he talked about his three sons, all devout Jews.

My own son called me a whore for voting against this bill . . .
He said for God's sake, don't let your vote be the one that
defeated this bill.

He said he had spent thirty-seven months in the Marines in
World War II, much of it in Pacific combat, "but this was worse
than anything." He represented a heavily Catholic district. "I
realize, Mr. Speaker, that I am terminating my career . . . but I
ask that my vote be changed from no to yes."[4] The assembly
was in chaos. Repeal leaders, tears streaming down their faces,
shouted and embraced. A few of us reached Connie Cook and
hugged and kissed her. Almost no one noticed that Perry
Duryea, the speaker, had cast his own vote at the end, making
the count seventy-six to seventy-three. The senate quickly
passed the same bill, and the governor signed it to take effect
on July 1, 1970.

The impact of the New York law was epochal. We had
achieved virtual repeal in one of the most important states in the
country. It would prove to be a shining example for other states.
Practically, New York could now take thousands of referrals
from the East Coast and even the Midwest. It could also be
assumed that the new law would influence the Supreme Court.
No one could surmise what molded the thinking of a Supreme
Court justice, but we had constantly stressed a woman's privacy
rights in our campaign, and federal and state courts had stressed
these rights in overthrowing anti-abortion laws. It was a cumu-
lative process. Since the Court had affirmed privacy in contraception only a few years before, the chances were that the justices would catch the mood of the nation and give equal
protection to privacy in abortion.

Meanwhile, NARAL had the complicated problem of making the New York law work. The main obstacle was raised by medical groups that demanded that abortions could only be done in hospitals, often requiring an overnight stay and sharply increased costs. We insisted that the procedure could be performed in free-standing clinics that met high medical standards, and that we run a training course for doctors and nurses to produce a core of professionals to staff them. The breakthrough came when we persuaded New York City's Health Services Administration to back us. Rev. Moody raised the money for a well-equipped clinic approved by the city. It would soon be taking applicants from dozens of states.

Planned Parenthood set up its own clinics. Other private clinics followed. Dangerous, back-alley abortions were replaced by abortions in safe, medical settings. Statistics showed an encouraging improvement in maternal health. In New York City in the nine months ending March 1972, the complication rate of pregnancy was cut from 12.4 to 6.3 per thousand cases.[5]

NARAL's strategy was to use the New York law to intensify the momentum. In the next target, Washington state, the Catholic church learned from its weaknesses in New York, and deluged voters with media and billboard ads. Although the bill passed the legislature and was approved by 56 to 44 percent in a referendum of the electorate, it limited abortion rights to the first seventeen weeks of pregnancy.

Everywhere legal teams stressed the privacy rights of women. In Illinois, where Dr. Lonny Myers, a NARAL vice president, headed the chapter, a three-judge federal panel ruled the state's abortion law unconstitutional. The wording of the decision, firmly linking abortion to contraception, declared that a

> woman's interest in privacy and control of her body is just as seriously interfered with by a law which prohibits abortion as it is by a law which prohibits the use of contraception.[6]

Building a strong sequence of decisions that was bound to influence the U. S. Supreme Court, federal courts in Connecticut and New Jersey and state supreme courts in Florida and Vermont also overturned old anti-abortion laws. The rapid legalization of abortion throughout the country may also have influenced the acceptance of cases by the U.S. Supreme Court. In 1966, statistics showed that only about six thousand legal abortions had been performed in hospitals, By the end of 1972, NARAL estimated there were at least six hundred thousand legal abortions performed nationwide, many in free-standing clinics.

Two cases—*Roe* v. *Wade* from Texas, and *Doe* v. *Bolton* from Georgia—seemed destined to reach the Supreme Court first.[7] The challenged Texas law, allowing abortion only to save the "life" of the woman, had already been overturned in lower federal courts. The state of Texas was now seeking a final decision. The Georgia law, stemming from hospital-imposed, "therapeutic abortion" committees, which resulted from a few moderate statutes passed after 1967, was also overturned by lower courts. Both cases were heard by the Court in 1971 before seven justices. In June 1972, the Court ordered a rehearing in the fall when President Nixon's two latest appointments—Lewis H. Powell and William H. Rehnquist—would be on the bench.

It was a tense period of preparation. The pro-choice side of the Texas case was being argued by Sarah Weddington, the Georgia case by Margie Pitts Hames. NARAL sent the chair of its legal committee, Cyril Means, to Washington to help. Planned Parenthood Federation sent its veteran counsel, Harriet Pilpel. For long hours, day after day, they ran "skull sessions" with Weddington and Hames trying to anticipate every question the justices might ask in court, honing the arguments for abortion rights to conform to the strict time limits imposed by the Court.

We arrived early, but long lines of anxious visitors hoping for a general admission seat had been forming all night. The court room seemed cavernous, almost oppressive in its marble severity. Weddington and Hames argued well, and afterwards we met to analyze the proceedings. No one knew when the decision would be handed down, and the months stretched on. Then on the morning of January 22, 1973, Fred Nathan from Pilpel's office phoned me excitedly. We had won by a seven-to-two vote. It was far stronger than we expected. Nathan added a final note of rejoicing. My 1966 book *Abortion* had been cited in the decision eight times, more than any other source.

Roe v. *Wade* abolished all restrictions on abortion in the first trimester of pregnancy except that it had to be performed by a licensed physician. In the second trimester up to the point of viability (set at twenty-four to twenty-eight weeks of pregnancy), the state could interfere only by regulating the qualifications of a doctor and the medical site for abortion if these factors were "reasonably related to maternal health." Although the Court seemed to give the medical profession final authority, there was no doubt that almost every woman would soon be able to find a clinic available for early abortion. In the incredibly short span of seven years, abortion rights had become national policy. I recalled that when my book was published and the debate launched, friends would slap me on the back and sympathize, "You're on the right track, of course, but it's going to take a hundred years."

It was probably the fastest social revolution in American history. What the movement had accomplished was to shake up the country as it had rarely been shaken since the anti-slavery era. A scrambled collection of seventy-five national and state groups had emerged from a few pioneers and had stayed glued together because they were convinced that abortion rights were not just central to women, but central to everything meaningful in life. The date of January 22 would be forever sacred to women and all progressive groups.

Still, I worried that the movement would slow down, believing that the struggle was finished. At a meeting of the national leadership from all organizations a few days later in New York, the champagne flowed in toast after toast. We were almost delirious. Everyone was ready to break up national and local networks that had been so pain-fully built. NARAL opposed any breakup. We could see trouble ahead and, unfortunately, we were right. The New York state law was saved a year later only by the governor's veto. The National Conference of Catholic Bishops would soon proclaim its "Pastoral Plan" and turn every parish in the country into a political machine to overthrow *Roe v. Wade*. Abortion clinics would also be invaded and burned to the ground. The country would be wracked by turmoil that had been unequaled in the last century.

NOTES

1. Founded in New York under a slightly different name, Catholics for a Free Choice is now an influential group in Washington, D.C., under the direction of Frances Kissling.

2. *William Lloyd Garrison: The Story of his Life, Told by His Children,* The Century Co., New York, 1885, vol. 1, p. 225.

3. *Eisenstadt* v. *Baird,* 405 U.S. 438, 31 L. Ed. 2d 349 (1972).

4. *New York Times,* April 10, 1970, p. 42; April 11, p. 17; April 12, p. 47. Author's interviews with George Michaels and family.

5. New York City Health Services Administration press release, February 20, 1971; April 25, 1972.

6. Despite a temporary injunction, 402 U.S. 903 (1971) vacated the injunction in the light of *Younger* v. *Harris,* 401 U.S. 37 (1971) and companion cases.

7. *Roe* v. *Wade,* 410 U.S. 113 (1973); *Doe* v. *Bolton,* 410 U.S. 179 (1973).

7

Perilous Years (1975–1990)

Success comes hard when there is little time to savor it. We were just beginning to build up our clinics around the country, with cities like Los Angeles and Chicago taking almost as many patients as New York. We had changed our name, keeping the acronym NARAL, but now calling ourselves the National Abortion Rights Action League. Suddenly we were on the defensive. The years of siege began. In 1975, the National Conference of Catholic Bishops announced its Pastoral Plan for Pro-Life Activities, making every parish priest and Catholic school a political weapon aimed at passing laws and winning judicial decisions that would outlaw abortion. Soon Catholic power would be augmented by an alliance with Protestant fundamentalists, an alliance cemented by the election of Ronald Reagan as president in 1980.

From 1975 on the National Right to Life committee began pushing Congress to pass a constitutional amendment that would overthrow or limit the effectiveness of *Roe* v. *Wade*. It forced through the Hyde Amendment (named for its sponsor, U.S. Rep. Henry Hyde, an Illinois Republican) that prohibited any federal funds being spent on Medicaid abortions. The poor, as usual, would suffer. Except for New York, California, and a handful of states, who paid the Medicaid bill themselves, the poor had to count on the charity of hospitals and clinics to cut their fees to a minimum. The irony was obvious. Opponents of abortion were constantly objecting to welfare subsidies for children of the poor, but they were equally against abortion for unwanted pregnancies.

Right to life committees began to hammer at prominent pro-choice candidates, one of the most noteworthy being U.S. Sen. Richard Clark, an Iowa Democrat, in 1978. Priests across the state attacked Clark by name, a potential violation of the U.S. tax code, which prohibits tax-exempt groups from supporting or attacking political candidates. On the Sunday before election day, hundreds of thousands of leaflets stigmatizing Clark for his support of abortion and the Equal Rights Amendment were distributed in church parking lots. Although polls had shown Clark 10 percentage points ahead, this last-minute deluge helped Clark's opponent win by twenty-five thousand votes.[1]

The Supreme Court, soon to be a conservative Reagan court, bolstered this trend. Newly appointed Justice Antonin Scalia openly announced he wanted to overthrow *Roe* v. *Wade*. Three major cases signaled this change. In *Harris* v. *McRae* in 1980, the Court ruled that federal and state governments were not required to fund even medically necessary abortions for welfare patients. *Webster* v. *Reproductive Health Services* in 1989 added regulations on clinics that increased costs and could put abortions out of reach for many patients. Although the basic right of abortion survived by one vote in *Planned Parenthood of Southeastern Pennsylvania* v. *Casey* in 1992, the Court approved a list of restrictions ranging from a twenty-four-hour waiting period to parental notification for minors.[2]

The most dangerous attack on abortion rights came from groups such as Operation Rescue and the Army of God. Their aim was to destroy or shut down clinics, or at least to block patients from entering them or doctors and staff from servicing them. These groups established picket lines around clinics, often scuffling with police and being arrested. Quickly out on bail, they moved on to other cities. They secured the addresses of doctors and patients from their license plates and attacked their homes. At a training camp in Florida, they taught their ultimate objective: the destruction of clinics and doctors.[3]

An Army of God pamphlet urged the firebombing of clinics. "The preferred method would be gasoline and matches. . . . Kerosene is great." Explosives are described as "a most wondrous method." The Army of God wants to eliminate doctors "by removing their hands, or at least their thumbs below the second digit."

All this meant a complete revolution in the role of clinics. They had to become fortresses as well as medical institutions. Often hiring expensive security advisory firms, they had to build impenetrable fences, employ guards, and recruit scores of activists each day to escort patients, doctors, and staff (who often wore bulletproof vests and arrived hidden on the floors of cars).

At vulnerable clinics, it became particularly hard to recruit doctors. In 83 percent of U.S. counties, there were no doctors to perform abortions. At medical schools, only 12 percent of obstetrics and gynecology programs required abortion training as part of the curriculum. Veterans like Dr. Jane Hodgson of Minnesota had to travel every week to nearby states to run their clinics. Abortion services were increasingly limited to larger cities. Thirty percent of American women of childbearing age had no access to abortion in their own counties, and states such as North and South Dakota had virtually no providers.

The political emphasis of the movement shifted radically. Whereas NARAL had once concentrated on a few states like New York to secure the most progressive legislation, the movement now had to build political machines almost everywhere to elect pro-choice candidates to the U.S. Congress and to state legislatures. Sophisticated techniques were used to identify prochoice voters, and an increasing number of campaigns hinged on this issue. In a New York suburb, the pressure on State Sen. Nicholas Spano, a Catholic and a Republican, became so intense he switched from opposition to abortion to prochoice in 1990. "I was elected to be a member of the Senate, not to impose my personal philosophy on all the people I represent," he insisted.[5] In New Jersey, a state that is 40 percent Catholic, U.S. Rep. Frank Pallone was elected as a Democrat on an anti-abortion platform in 1988. But as polls showed the impact of prochoice organizing, Pallone reversed his stand.

The political campaign drew all branches of the abortion movement into a common front. The Planned Parenthood Federation of America had once drawn largely on suburban housewives. However, under the direction of Faye Wattleton, an attractive black woman whose debating prowess made her a star on television and radio, Planned Parenthood's chain of clinics became an aggressive force. They took constant, nationwide newspaper ads in defense of *Roe* v. *Wade.* They enlarged their lobbying office in Washington, D.C.

The National Organization for Women (NOW) soon made abortion rights its main focus. Under the dynamic presidencies of Eleanor Smeal, Molly Yard, and Patricia Ireland, it built up its local chapters as political centers and ran the two most successful feminist marches in U.S. history. As testimony to the anger roused by the erosion of *Roe* v. *Wade,* at least half a million people from across the country poured through the streets of Washington, D.C., in the spring of 1989.

Molly Yard would be felled by a stroke in May 1991, working at her desk late at night at the NOW office. Severely paralyzed, her speech impaired, she would regain the booming strength of her voice a year later, and begin accepting speaking engagements. Smeal would go on to found the Feminist Majority, an organization taking responsibility for clinic defense around the country.

Admittedly, there were often strains between these dominant personalities, particularly when Kate Michelman became head of NARAL, and organizations in New Jersey, and Westchester County, New York, under the leadership of Polly Rothstein, decided to operate on their own. But the most severe strain came in late 1974 as my term as chair of NARAL's board was close to ending.

A growing faction in NARAL believed that the "old guard" militants, which I represented, had outlived their usefulness. It was thought that we were pushing NARAL into too many confrontations, mainly with the Catholic church. We were hesitant to concentrate on congressional lobbying and move the office to Washington. We had always seen NARAL as a coalition of state and local groups rather than as a membership organization. Although we had agreed to build up membership a few years before by incorporating the Ohio membership into NARAL, and probably had about 25,000 members at the time, we were reluctant to turn NARAL into a massive bureaucracy. The final break came at the national meeting in November 1974. The militants still held a majority of votes on the board, but the new board would be elected by the membership, and for the first time, two competing slates opposed each other.

Once I knew almost every member personally. Now with thousands of new members, the militants could not afford a mailing, whereas our opponents, through a few rich officers, could finance a direct-mail campaign. Although I was re-elected chair for a sixth and final term, most of the militants were voted out. I had become a figurehead, an outsider in an organization I had helped to build painfully, through many sleepless years.

The most devastating blow at the 1974 meeting was the defection of Dr. Bernard Nathanson. He had been chair of the medical committee from the very beginning, and closely allied with the militants. He had put together and run Rev. Howard Moody's remarkable clinic after the passage in 1970 of New York's law legalizing abortion. I was on the podium at the contentious board meeting when someone rushed up to me with a copy of the *New England Journal of Medicine* of November 28, 1974. It contained a bombshell article written by Nathanson. After years of commitment, he had totally reversed his stand and proclaimed his unequivocal opposition to abortion rights. Dismay and anger shook the audience. The article would not only do immeasurable harm to NARAL but to the militants as well. There were immediate demands for his ouster, but before it could be formalized a few weeks later, he resigned.

Nathanson quickly became the darling of the fundamentalist and Catholic extremists. He was flooded with speaking engagements by such groups as the National Right to Life Committee, and represented them on radio and TV. The media was always receptive of controversy. Who could better rouse a storm than a doctor who had helped to found NARAL, but deserted his long-time allies to achieve his peculiar form of personal salvation?

Nathanson would eventually publish a book, *Aborting America,* detailing the story of his conversion. It was a strange and violent work marred by factual errors, particularly involving my life. He would increase his attacks on abortion rights by producing and narrating a film called "The Silent Scream." Its purpose was to prove that an aborted fetus could feel pain and terror. It concluded with the right-to-life thesis that a fetus in the womb was nothing less than a living person. Almost all Nathanson's claims were refuted at a meetings of prominent doctors and scientists at the Planned Parenthood Federation. Their report was widely circulated, and I summed up their conclusions in an op-ed piece published in New York *Newsday* on April 25, 1985.

One of the main factors harming Nathanson's stability was his father, a successful obstetrician-gynecologist he envied. Nathanson's father was a determined opponent of abortion. The dispute between them became so severe, the father refused to speak to the son for years. The son was shut out from family gatherings.

In the last years of his father's life, the son must have

yearned to return to his embrace. His rapprochement with his father was obviously stronger than his link to his old allies.

Nathanson probably realized that as our militant faction lost control of NARAL in 1974, he would soon lose his power base. When my term as chair expired, he would undoubtedly have been dropped as head of the medical committee. If he lost his heroic status in NARAL, he may have figured he could regain it as the new hero of the religious right. Nathanson contended in his book that he had shown me a draft of his *New England Journal of Medicine* article. Yet not I, the NARAL leadership, nor Moody had any inkling of his intentions. Admittedly, there were a few who mistrusted him. I probably should have listened to them more attentively. But we had gone through a similar struggle years before to oust the legal committee chair, and I had no stomach for another.

The most drastic change in NARAL was the move of its headquarters to Washington, D.C. With the increasing struggle over abortion rights, its membership expanded to almost 350,000 by 1982. For five years, I had made all substantial decisions. Although the presidency and chair of NARAL would now be held by skilled and committed women like Robin Duke and Margie Pitts Hames, their roles increasingly concentrated on fundraising and media appearances. Real control would pass to the executive director and later president, Kate Michelman. A huge budget allowed for a paid staff of lawyers and public relations experts, a luxury we never had. In my first visit to the new office in a prime Washington building, I was startled by the thick carpets and regal furniture that looked more like the headquarters for a major corporation than for a radical movement. But perhaps NARAL was right in surrounding itself in corporate trappings. It now had to be a key player on Capitol Hill.

In 1975, when most of the old guard was rotated off the NARAL board, we decided to form a new type of organization called Abortion Rights Mobilization (ARM). We wanted to continue the strategy of political confrontation. We wanted to tackle emergencies that national groups usually avoided. We wanted a highly efficient board of about thirty members, able to move so fast that a project could be launched with just an hour's worth of phone calls to the executive committee. Almost all NARAL veterans joined us, including Dr. Edgar Keemer, Lana Phelan, former Congressman Charles Porter, former Manhattan Borough President Percy Sutton, and Edith Tiger. I was chosen to be president.

We pared expenses to the bone and rented a small office. Occasionally we had an executive director, but most of the time a few board members and I, all unsalaried, handled the work. When we raised money, we could assure a foundation we were giving "more bang for the buck" than any other organization.

Our commitment to fast action was tested during the Georgia elections a few years ago when NOW told us that pro-choice candidates were in serious trouble. Drawing on some of the tragic letters I had received from women seeking abortion before legalization, we wrote vivid radio "spots," assembled experienced actors and actresses, cut the spots and booked time in Atlanta and other cities all within two days.

Nothing was ever put together faster than the "Italian project." In 1981, the Italian Parliament passed a law legalizing abortion, which then had to be approved by a majority of voters through a national referendum. In a unique campaign, particularly for an ostensibly Catholic country, feminist members of Parliament, health officials, and the women's movement convinced the country to support abortion rights by a two-thirds margin. ARM thought that if the story could be brought to members of Congress and to Catholic voters, it might help to dilute right-wing religious opposition here. Running up enormous long-distance phone bills, I managed to track down six or seven women members of Parliament and persuade them to come to Washington (all expenses paid) in the next week. For good measure, they brought along a rebel Catholic priest who had worked hard on the referendum.

U.S. Rep. Patricia Schroeder (D-Colorado) chaired the meeting in a large House of Representatives hearing room. Members of Congress and their staffs, as well as the press, crowded in.

The Italian officials presented their case with power and simplicity and repeated the presentation before New York officials a day later. I have always believed that a Catholic country can quickly grasp the importance of abortion rights when it is stripped of theology and focused on a woman's health and personal survival. Spain certainly proved this, legalizing abortion just sixteen years after the Franco dictatorship.

In 1980, the counterattack against *Roe* v. *Wade* intensified. We began to realize that the Catholic church had an exceptional advantage since it used tax-exempt funds and the facilities of its parishes to attack, and defeat, prochoice political candidates. This process was hastened by the alliance between fundamentalists in the "Moral Majority" and the Catholic bishops. A new and explosive fact had been introduced into political campaigns, not just the fusion of powerful religious groups, but the illegal use of religious money to fight against abortion.

Congress in Sec. 501-c-3 of the U.S. tax code strictly forbade religious organizations with tax exemption to "participate in, or intervene in [including the publishing or distribution of statements], any political campaign on behalf of [or in opposition to] any candidate for public office." The advantage given to religious groups skirting the law had already been demonstrated in many races, including the distribution of political leaflets on church property that helped in the defeat of Sen. Clark. It was the Internal Revenue Service's responsibility to enforce the law. One of the rare times it did so was in the case of the *Christian Century,* a small Protestant journal published in Chicago, which editorially supported Lyndon Johnson for president in 1964. The IRS removed its tax exemption, for three years.[6]

We were a small organization with a tiny budget bringing a federal lawsuit against the Catholic church, one of the nation's great power centers. Few people had dared to tangle with the Catholic church in court, but it was the kind of gamble ARM had been made for. Our first step was to collect a few pieces of evidence of Catholic church violations, and to mail them to the IRS requesting that it take appropriate action.

We got no answer. We mailed them a second time, and still no answer.

We then had to look for an ideal lawyer. Eventually we found Marshall Beil, a graduate of Swarthmore and Harvard Law School, who had worked as a volunteer for the ACLU. He was young, aggressive, and dedicated to our case.

We needed stronger proof of Church violations. What a

religious group could not do was to either support or attack political candidates, using the pulpit, tax-exempt telephones, duplicating machines, or any religious property. Under the First Amendment guarantee of free speech, religious groups could discuss all issues, including political issues, from the pulpits or in any media. Our evidence had to be in church bulletins, newspapers, or letters on church stationery, since it would be more complicated to have witnesses testify about verbal violations.

As far back as 1970, parishes in Maryland distributed a letter urging Catholic voters to support a list of candidates for the U.S. House of Representatives and the State Assembly, all of whom were opposed to abortion. Soon thereafter, parish church bulletins in Westchester County, New York, attacked prochoice candidates for the county legislature. The attacks intensified in 1980, ranging from Pennsylvania and Illinois, to Michigan and Minnesota parishes. In a tight race in Massachusetts that year, a Worcester monsignor attacked a congressional candidate in a letter ordered to be read from pulpits. The most blatant violation of the law was an editorial on May 2, 1980, in *Today's Catholic,* the official diocesan newspaper of San Antonio, Texas. Directly challenging the government in its headline, "To the IRS—NUTS!!!" it went on to support Ronald Reagan for president and favored a long list of candidates for the U.S. Senate and House of Representatives.

We collected evidence from fundamentalist churches as well, one example being the pastor of a Baptist church in Tampa, Florida, who checked off the antiabortion candidates on a sample ballot, printed it, and distributed it to his congregation.

Whereas this evidence might appear to be unshakable at trial, we knew from the outset that the main problem for Beil and his legal staff would be the issue of "standing," or the right to sue. This was a peculiar hurdle. To secure standing, the U.S. Supreme Court required that a "plaintiff must allege personal injury fairly traceable to the defendant's allegedly unlawful conduct and likely to be redressed by that requested relief." The Court has traditionally insisted on an "injury in fact," not one that was "abstract" or "hypothetical."

To meet these requirements, we put together a range of plaintiffs, certain that at least one group would qualify. We had a number of prochoice Protestant and Jewish clergy. They asserted that like many Catholic priests, they would have liked to support or attack candidates. But since they obeyed the law, they lost political effectiveness and suffered specific personal injury. Another group of church-going Catholics asserted that they were personally injured because their religious contributions were being used against their will for direct, antiabortion political intervention. Similarly, Protestant and Jewish worshippers argued that they were damaged because their contributions to churches and synagogues that obeyed the law would have no political impact in the abortion conflict.

The Catholic strategy was shrewd. Knowing that we had ample evidence to win at trial, possibly resulting in a loss of tax exemption, the church's lawyers hammered relentlessly at the standing issue. The church was not only represented by the firm of Edward Bennet Williams, which was highly influential in government circles, but by its own in-house staff, ironically paid with tax-exempt money.

The lawsuit went before Judge Robert L. Carter of the U.S. District Court in Manhattan, who ruled that the defendant must also be the IRS because of its responsibility for enforcing the law. Thus we now confronted the legal strength of the U.S. attorney's office, paid, of course, by public taxes. Judge Carter immediately gave us standing. But the opposition lawyers twisted and wriggled for years through every loophole in the law, even refusing to turn over to us documents that were part of the routine process of "discovery," essential for going to trial. Each time Judge Carter ruled in our favor, the opposition continued its delaying tactics by going to the U.S. Court of Appeals, where we were upheld again. Judge Carter branded these obstructions a "wasteful charade."

It was not until May 8, 1986, that this dismal process had run its course, and Judge Carter issued a momentous opinion. Punishing the Catholic bishops for refusing to give us the discovery documents, he held the U.S. Catholic Conference and the National Conference of Catholic Bishops in contempt of court and fined each organization $50,000 a day until they obeyed the court's order. The church's lawyers, the judge ruled angrily, "have willfully misled the court and the plaintiffs and have made a travesty of the court process."

It was an occasion for rejoicing after years of labor. *Time* magazine called our lawsuit a "major constitutional test case on the limits of mixing religion and politics." Professor Alan Dershowitz, a Harvard Law School constitutional expert, concluded it was "completely unprecedented for a large established religious group to be found in contempt."[7]

The opposition lawyers, convinced they could only win on the standing issue, dragged us once more to the U.S. Court of Appeals. Now we had our first setback. One judge on the three-judge panel, which had upheld us before, reversed position. We were denied standing in a two-to-one vote, the panel ruling that our plaintiffs were not "competitive advocates" because they did not compete with the Catholic church in the political arena.

We actually went to the U.S. Supreme Court twice. In 1988, the Catholic church challenged the jurisdiction of Judge Carter for holding it in contempt. The Supreme Court approved its right to challenge. In 1990, we had to go to the Supreme Court again on standing. It was our last resort. Marshall Beil had worked for years on research and briefs. With no staff, I had struggled to raise the money to pay our bills. We had forced a critical issue into judicial and public scrutiny: insisting that the church's political intervention was a government subsidy for established religion and violated the Establishment Clause of the First Amendment.

The enormity of our constitutional case had now been reduced to the seemingly unimportant factor of standing. Ten years of litigation would depend on it, and we lost. The Supreme Court denied us standing for the reason that ARM and its plaintiffs were not in competition with the Catholic church.[8] Our case was over.

I have always been convinced that the Supreme Court wanted to avoid a decision on one of the more sensitive aspects of religion and the First Amendment, and used standing to get rid of us. Some of the most acute legal scholars have told us that the Court acted inconsistently with its precedents, and this viewpoint was summed up in an exhaustive analysis in the Fordham Law School's *Review,* an institution, incidentally, run by the Catholic church. This paper compared our arguments with those of the *Fulani* case decided not long before by the same appeals court. Fulani, a minor party candidate, challenged the tax exemption of the League of Women Voters for being excluded from a public debate. Both cases had "similar factual situations," the paper stressed. Yet Fulani got standing; we didn't. Moreover, federal courts in the District of Columbia found that when plaintiffs suffered unfairly from the subsidization of their competitors' voices, this diminished the plaintiffs' ability to affect the political process.

Despite our bitter defeat from what we considered an irrational application of the law, the ARM case would have an enormous impact on practical politics. On two occasions, the last before the 1992 elections, the U.S. Catholic Conference issued a strong memo warning all bishops that "political campaign activity is strictly prohibited." Pointing out that dismissal of the ARM case in no way diminished the restrictions of the U.S. tax code, the U.S.Catholic Conference banned financial support to any candidate, political action committee, or political party, including supporting or opposing any candidate "via a sermon or parish bulletin, through an editorial position in a Catholic newspaper, or through distribution of filled-in sample ballots."[9] We may never have gone to trial on the evidence, but in practical terms, the Catholic Conference had given us everything we wanted. If its warning to all bishops was heeded, and separation of church and state was maintained, the long struggle had been well worth it.

The Internal Revenue Service finally acted to enforce the U.S. tax code. On January 19, 1995, it took away the tax exemption of the Church at Pierce Creek in Vestal, New York, a nondenominational Christian church, for direct opposition to a political candidate. On October 30, 1992, in an advertisement a week before the presidential election in *USA Today* and the

Washington Times, Bill Clinton was attacked for advocating abortion, homosexuality, and distribution of condoms in public schools. The article demanded, "Do we really want as president . . . a man of this character who supports this type of behavior?" It concluded, "How then can we vote for Bill Clinton?" Although the American Center for Law and Justice, a group funded by fundamentalist leader Pat Robertson, went to federal court in the District of Columbia to overturn the IRS decision, it seemed as if ARM's years of pressure on the IRS had had positive, concrete results.[10]

NOTES

1. Author's interviews with Mary Jean Collins and Monica McFadden (National Organization for Women).

2. *Harris* v. *McRae,* 448 U.S. 297 (1980); *Webster* v. *Reproductive Health Services,* 488 U.S. 1003 (1989); *Planned Parenthood of Southeastern Pennsylvania* v. *Casey,* 112 Sup. Ct. 2791, 120 L. Ed. 2d, 29 June 1992.

3. Files of Feminist Majority, Arlington, Virginia. Author's interviews with Dallas Blanchard and Susan Hill.

4. Carolyn Westhoff, "Abortion Training in Residency Programs," *Journal of the American Medical Women's Association,* vol. 49, no. 3 (September/October 1994), pp. 150–52.

5. *Pro Choice* newsletter, Westchester Coalition for Legal Abortion, Mamaroneck, N.Y., June 1990, p. 1.

6. Letter of October 19, 1967, from U.S. Treasury Department, Internal Revenue Service, District Director, Chicago, Illinois, to Christian Century Foundation.

7. *Time* magazine, May 19, 1986, vol. 127, no. 19.

8. ARM lawsuit: *Abortion Rights Mobilization, Inc.* v. *Regan,* 544 F.

Supp. p. 471 (S.D.N.Y. 1982); *Abortion Rights Mobilization, Inc. v. Regan,* 603 F. Supp. p. 970 (S.D.N.Y. 1985); *Abortion Rights Mobilization, Inc. v. Baker,* 110 F.D.R. 337 (S.D.N.Y. 1986); *In Re U.S. Catholic Conference,* 824 F. 2d 156 (2d Cir. 1987); *U.S. Catholic Conference v. Abortion Rights Mobilization, Inc.,* 487 U.S. 72, 108 S. Ct. 2268, 101 L. Ed. 2d 69 (1988); *In Re U.S. Catholic Conference,* 885 F. 2d 1020 (2d Cir. 1989); *Abortion Rights Mobilization, Inc. v. U.S. Catholic Conference,* 495 U.S. 918, 110 S. Ct. 1946, 109 L. Ed. 2d 309 (1990).

9. *New York Times,* August 1, 1988; Church and State, September 1992, p. 3.

10. *Branch Ministries d/b/a/ the Church at Pierce Creek* v. *Margaret M. Richardson,* 1: 95 CV00724, U.SD.C., D.C., April 17, 1995.

8

RU 486: The Next Essential Step

When the French government approved RU 486 for general use in September 1988, and the French minister of health hailed the new abortion pill as the "moral property of women,"[1] Abortion Rights Mobilization grasped its momentous consequences. ARM's board decided to concentrate on getting it into the United States. I decided to write a book titled *RU 486* to bring the pill's significance to the public. Here was a scientific advance that could eliminate the need for surgery, move the setting of abortion to the privacy of a doctor's office, and keep reproductive choice totally within the control of doctors and their patients. Opponents of abortion could not picket or raid every doctor's office in America. With clinics under a rising threat of firebombing, and clinic doctors targets of assassination, RU 486 had the potential of diminishing the furious clashes over abortion.

Two of the pill's important attributes are its effectiveness and its safety. It has induced abortion (followed by a dose of prostaglandin) in 96 percent of at least two hundred thousand cases. It has comparatively few side effects. It works by producing a heavy menstrual flow, virtually equivalent to a woman's normal period. There is no sign of an actual person, nothing resembling a possible finger or toe. It would be hard to differentiate the pill's action from a "miscarriage." An objective observer could scarcely claim that anything has been "killed." Referring to fetal tissue at this early stage, Dr. David Grimes, who ran early tests on RU 486 at the University of Southern California, explains, "You can't even find it."[2]

It is hardly surprising that 77 percent of French women who have undergone both vacuum abortion and RU 486 abortion favored the pill.[3] RU 486 has "de-medicalized" and humanized abortion. It eliminates what one French woman called "surgery aggression." Another pointed out, "There is no intrusion on the integrity of the body." An American woman in Dr. Grimes's tests concluded, "What I liked was taking care of myself, not being in the hands of doctors. It brought a sense of knowledge and control, a positive existential experience."[4] RU 486 helps a woman feel that she is far more than flesh on a table subject to medical routine. It guarantees her sensitivity and makes her master of her life.

In contrast to the one-step process of vacuum abortion, RU 486 involves more time and complexities. In France the patient must be checked by a doctor to be certain her pregnancy is under seven weeks (nine weeks in Britain and elsewhere). Then the patient is given RU 486 (600 milligrams in one or more pills) and two days later a dose of prostaglandin to intensify the action. In the final visit, a medical exam confirms that abortion has been completed successfully and that bleeding has stopped.

The principal annoyances women experience from RU 486 combined with prostaglandin are uterine contractions, light nausea, and diarrhea, which may continue for a few hours. "Most women have no pain at all," concludes Dr. Elisabeth Aubeny in her French study.[5] In a multinational study done by the World Health Organization, only 7.6 percent of the cases had enough pain to require narcotic analgesics. In a British study, 23 percent needed a painkiller.

Medical complications from RU 486 have been rare. In France, two cardiovascular complications involved women thirty-five and thirty-eight years of age, one a heavy smoker, the other under severe psychological stress. Both women recovered completely. Doctors henceforth avoided giving the pill to older women, particularly to women with a predisposition to cardiovascular risks. Unfortunately, one French death has been attributed to RU 486. Statistically, every drug has a risk, and one death in over 200,000 RU 486 cases is a far lower rate than 1.1 deaths for 100,000 penicillin doses, which the public has been taking routinely for decades. Moreover, the patient was hypertensive and a heavy smoker and according to RU 486 standards should never have been accepted for treatment. With careful screening, such a tragic accident should never happen again.

It is a remarkable testament to the versatility of RU 486 that the compound not only has been used for abortion in France, Britain, Sweden (with U.S. tests now in progress), but that it may well become an important contraceptive. It could eliminate the possibility of pregnancy with a woman never knowing if she were pregnant or not. Another advantage is that as few as twelve doses a year may be the maximum required, thus limiting the impact on a woman's hormonal system, in contrast to about 240 doses of the present birth control pills. By inhibiting progesterone, RU 486 prevents preparation of the uterus for implantation of the egg.[7]

A problem still to be solved involves the possibility of double-bleeding. A woman taking RU 486 as a contraceptive would not only bleed at that time but possibly again at the time of her normal end of cycle. Some researchers did not encounter this problem, and the chances of double-bleeding are greatly diminished by taking RU 486 two or three days before expected menses. Dr. Marc Bygdeman of the Karolinska Hospital in Stockholm, who initiated the research on combining prostaglandin with RU 486, concludes, "We think that if the pill is taken around twenty-four hours after ovulation it can prevent pregnancy."[8]

Already proven in European tests, RU 486 has become a critical factor in helping women through difficult deliveries. The drug may reduce the number of cesarean sections as an alternative for those deliveries. At least one of every four U.S. births seems to require a cesarean section. Because of its antiprogesterone effect, RU 486 makes the uterus contract and thus speeds the opening of the cervix.[9]

In other aspects of delivery, RU 486 facilitates the extraction of ectopic embryos, abnormal fetuses, and fetuses that have died in the uterus. Further, RU 486 can be an essential supplement to late first trimester abortions done by the suction method. By dilating the cervix, it can diminish the breaking of muscle fibers and cervical damage, which sometimes results from the suction power of a vacuum machine or the internal probing of the machine's tube. Throughout the third trimester of pregnancy, RU 486 and prostaglandin may become an alternative to surgery to end a pregnancy as a result of a malformed fetus or because the mother's health is threatened. This therapy in late pregnancy could be generally less risky than the kinds of surgery now performed.[10]

At the National Institutes of Health, located in Bethesda, Maryland, RU 486 has already proved valuable in treating Cushing's syndrome, a life-threatening condition that results from excessive production of the adrenal gland hormone cortisol and the abnormalities it causes in body tissue and blood chemistry. Surgery had always been the standard treatment.

But a National Institutes of Health report concludes:

> Surgery is particularly hazardous for patients with Cushing's syndrome, and the use of RU 486 to correct the abnormalities caused by excessive cortisol before surgery should make the procedure safer and improve outcome.[11]

In another promising area of treatment, RU 486 has been used for meningioma, a primary tumor of the membrane that surrounds the brain and that often causes impaired mental function. "Brain tumors contain progesterone receptors," explains Dr. Daniel Philibert of the Roussel company, the French developer of the pill. Dr. Steven Grunberg of the University of Vermont reports that RU 486 "happens to have the hormonal effect that we're looking for to treat this tumor." After giving the compound to scores of patients, Grunberg concludes, "We're very excited and encouraged."[12]

Like all scientific breakthroughs, RU 486 was the result of an evolutionary process, a chain of building blocks of research dating back many decades. It was the result of a research team at the Roussel company and the work on "receptors" by Dr. Étienne-Émile Baulieu, a professor at Bicêtre Hospital in Paris. The first insight came from one of Baulieu's mentors, Dr. Gregory Pincus, of the Worcester Foundation for Experimental Biology in Massachusetts, who theorized in 1962 that antiprogestins could act on specific receptors in the uterus and stop the growth of the egg. Baulieu had met Pincus the year before and was impressed by his research on the birth control pill.

Thirty years before, chemists had established the chemical structure of sex hormones or steroids, including estradiol, progesterone, and testosterone. But natural hormones from animals were inordinately expensive, and in the early 1940s, Professor Russell E. Marker of Pennsylvania State University discovered a far cheaper way to synthesize them. The newly formed Syntex company became the leading supplier of synthetic steroids. RU 486 is antagonistic to the sex hormone progesterone. By occupying the space in the progesterone receptor without activating it, RU 486 impedes progesterone from entering the receptor. Instead of inducing the usual hormone responses, RU 486 stops them.

Progesterone plays a central role in establishing pregnancy. It prepares the uterus for implantation and nurtures the egg. A specific receptor in the uterus receives the progesterone. If fertilization occurs, progesterone production helps the new embryo lodge in the lining of the uterus, promotes development of the placenta, and de-creases the chance of expulsion of the embryo. RU 486 thus "barricades" the receptor. When RU 486 penetrates the receptor, it binds to it and deceives it, working against implantation. The developing placenta and embryo detach from the uterine lining. There are increased contractions that dislodge and expel the embryo. Through the seventh to ninth weeks of the woman's cycle, RU 486 brings about an early abortion because of diminished progesterone and bleeding that results from shedding of the endometrium (the mucous membrane lining the uterus).

When Baulieu started progesterone receptor research around 1970, no one knew how the receptor really functioned. A research group at Roussel headed by Dr. Georges Teutsch was trying to develop the best molecule close to cortisone (fortunately similar to progesterone), a molecule that would bind to and block the receptors without triggering the normal hormonal response. A steroid or sex hormone is like a key, and an antisteroid can prevent the key from opening the lock. Whereas Teutsch and his group were making a fake key that would fit the lock, Baulieu's work was defining the shape of the lock. By occupying the lock, a fake key would impede the real key from opening the door.

In a 1975 paper, Baulieu urged more research on the "relationship between receptor concentration and hormone action." Over the next few years, Teutsch tested hundreds of compounds. "We wanted one with the highest binding qualities," he recalled.[13] All told, nine hundred compounds may have been screened. In 1980, Teutsch told a meeting of Roussel executives that some compounds had real potential as a new abortifacient. The compound Roussel finally decided to promote was called mifepristone, or RU 486. The company applied for a patent in 1980, and it was approved the next year.

Baulieu approached Professor Walter Hermann of Geneva's University Hospital, an old friend, and got him to search for female volunteers. Eleven pregnant women agreed to participate in the first test, and nine aborted quickly. In a test sample of a hundred women in 1986, RU 486 achieved a success rate of 85 percent. As an international network of scientists, including the World Health Organization, set up their own test programs, Dr. Bygdeman in Stockholm demonstrated that a small dose of prostaglandins (substances in body tissue that act like hormones) would make the uterus react more strongly than would RU 486 alone. Bleeding would be decreased. Abortion often occurred within a few hours. As a result of the combined dosages, the success rate was quickly raised to 96 per cent.[14] Studies showed that no other receptors were affected except for a weak anticortisone action. Consequently, women have been able to conceive again shortly after undergoing an RU 486 abortion.

After all studies were submitted to the French Ministry of Health, the pill was officially approved for the public on September 23, 1988. Cardinal Jean-Marie Lustiger of Paris and other bishops immediately branded RU 486 as a "chemical weapon" against the unborn, and the church organized a protest march through Paris that drew barely two thousand people. Still, the Roussel company withdrew the pill from the market until Claude Evin, the minister of health, reversed the order in late October. According to law, he had considerable power over Roussel. Not only did the government own 36 percent of the company, but it could remove the company's license and award it to another manufacturer if a drug that had proved safe and effective was withdrawn from public use. Evin announced that his decision had been made "out of concern for the public health and what this pill means for women."[15]

The possibility of manufacturing and distributing RU 486 in the United States, however, was enmeshed in political fury. The Roussel company was controlled by Hoechst of Germany, its majority shareholder. Hoechst made almost $7 billion annual sales in the United States, and was appalled at the possibility that its plants and products could be picketed by the Catholic-fundamentalist alliance. Not only was Hoechst's president, Wolfgang Hilger, a devout Roman Catholic and opposed to abortion, but the company was the successor to I.G. Farben, which had produced the gas for Hitler's concentration camp death chambers. Hilger feared the "death pill" tag that opponents were already giving RU 486.

America's Catholic-fundamentalist alliance quickly made RU 486 the object of its wrath. U.S. Rep. Robert Dornan (R-California) introduced legislation to prohibit RU 486 and prevent its approval by the Food and Drug Administration (FDA). The National Right to Life Committee labeled the pill a "death drug" and fundamentalists called it a "human pesticide."[16] Cooperating with these extremists, Presidents Ronald Reagan and George Bush, both strong anti-abortion advocates, stopped all RU 486 research at the National Institutes of Health, and forced the FDA to put the drug on the proscribed list, thereby blocking its entry into the country.

The vehemence of extremism went far beyond RU 486. In its campaign against contraception and sexual practices it wanted prohibited, *Christianity Today*, a major fundamentalist journal, demanded the "validity of virginity, the management of masturbation." Joseph Scheidler, head of the Pro-Life Action League, branded contraception as "disgusting, people using each other for pleasure." State Sen. Jim West (R-Spokane) introduced a bill into the Washington state legislature that would make it a crime for people under the age of eighteen to engage in sex, including "heavy petting."[17]

It would take a highly focused campaign to counter such extremism, and prestigious medical groups were the logical starting point. In a March 1990 resolution, the California Medical Association voted overwhelmingly for the admission of RU 486 into the country. Patients should have a choice of treatments, the association stressed, adding:

> It is in keeping with basic medical standards to avoid surgical procedures whenever an equally effective noninvasive alternative is available.

Soon after, the American Medical Association's House of Delegates, representing 290,000 doctors nationwide, and the American College of Obstetricians and Gynecologists took almost identical positions.[18] It was hard to deal with a small block of extremist voters, estimated at 15 percent of the electorate, who exerted a great deal of influence on the Reagan and Bush administrations and on enough members of Congress to block RU 486 from admission to the U.S. population. Much of their power came from a fear among politicians that an election can be lost by five hundred to a thousand votes from a highly organized pressure group. Under the sway of media demagogues like the Rev. Pat Robertson, the right-wing alliance had learned how to nail down its votes. Reagan and Bush counted on its support. It seemed to be a rigid and unshakable opponent.

The abortion movement's basic strategy for reaching extremists was through the media, and we constantly tried to promote editorial support. Calling the advantages of the pill "so clear-cut that it cannot long be denied American women," the *Boston Globe* insisted, "It is unrealistic to envision women throughout the world having access to RU 486, while American women are denied it." The *Washington Post* urged that "neither this government nor the French manufacturer should let political considerations delay the [approval] process." After pointing out that "clearly, then, there is an American market for RU 486," the *New York Times* asked, "Now where is the marketer?"[19]

The weakness of this approach, of course, was that we were mainly supported by big city newspapers, and not reaching the towns of the South and Southwest, the heartland of extremism. The best route to these areas were the radio talk shows. Doing them from New York by telephone, I suffered through the screaming invectives and biblical quotations hurled at me in the hope that I might reach a few wavering minds. My favorite ploy was to ask a call-in opponent whether he or she wanted to cut abortions in half in a year. The answer, naturally, was affirmative. Then I suggested: Join us in a mutual campaign. Join us in making contraceptives widely available, join us in bringing sex education to the schools, and we can almost certainly decrease abortions quickly. The reaction was usually a dead silence. Extremists, unfortunately, were almost always as much opposed to birth control as they were to abortion.

All these obstacles to the admission of RU 486 to the United States were linked to the negative position of the Roussel company itself. Roussel had to apply to the FDA to start the approval process, and it consistently refused. Its fears went far deeper than potential boycotts of Hoechst products here or a political backlash from extremists. The company's greatest fear was a highly organized boycott by Catholic hospitals, which control approximately one-third of all hospital beds in the

United States and represent 640 out of 3,289 nonprofit, non-governmental institutions. If these Catholic hospitals refused as a block to buy any Hoechst-Roussel products, the company's sales could be severely reduced. Such a situation may be an unfortunate example of religious morality taking over medical practice, but the implication of these statistics in business terms is all too clear.

The obvious strategy for the abortion movement was to launch every possible pressure on Roussel. Delegations of women flew repeatedly to Paris to meet with the president of the company. Molly Yard, president of the National Organization for Women, and Dr. Allan Rosenfield, former chairman of the Planned Parenthood Federation, lobbied Roussel on behalf of their delegations. Eleanor Smeal, president of the Fund for a Feminist Majority, brought petitions signed by 125,000 Americans urging immediate introduction of the pill. Dr. Baulieu, a leading developer of the pill, insisted that the "key to the future of RU 486 lies in the United States." Feminists set up picket lines outside Hoechst plants here. At the national women's marches in Washington, D.C., speaker after speaker hammered at the importance of RU 486. Yet nothing had any effect. In March 1990, Edward Norton, spokesman for Hoechst-Roussel Pharmaceuticals of New Jersey, defined the company's position:

> We've been petitioned, we've been yelled at, and we've been telephoned by everybody. But our formal position hasn't changed in two years, and I don't expect it to change.

Ariel Mouttet, head of international marketing for Roussel in Paris, announced in July 1990: "Selling in the United States is out of the question at the moment."[20] By 1990, it had become gospel to the women's movement and the family planning movement that RU 486 was pivotal to abortion rights. It was not just a question of the privacy of abortion in a doctor's office, or making abortion available in many areas lacking services. The core issue was giving abortion rights a new impetus, gaining new ground, rousing the country for a critical challenge.

Despite the support of a few Republicans like Gov. Pete Wilson of California, we faced the constant threat of President Bush's partnership with the Catholic-fundamentalist alliance and the anti-abortion damage of the Republican platform. The Supreme Court was dubious, and in the *Pennsylvania* case the very principle of abortion rights was upheld by only a single vote. Abortion rights were in crisis.

What decisive solution could be found? Abortion Rights Mobilization decided to take on the responsibility of RU 486. We were a small organization, but innovative and tough. We had developed shrewd strategies in the past that targeted an objective, and then worked out the means to harness positive public opinion and approval and reach it. This was the kind of fast-breaking challenge we welcomed, and it immediately became our sole priority.

NOTES

1. *Baltimore Sun,* October 29, 1988, p. 1A.
2. *Detroit Free Press,* November 22, 1988, p. B 2; telephone interview with author July 16, 1990.

3. Author's interview with Elisabeth Aubeny, Paris, February 4, 1990.

4. *Le Nouvel Observateur,* March 30, 1988, p. 130; American woman interview by phone requested anonymity.

5. Elisabeth Aubeny interview, Paris, February 4, 1990.

6. Paul F. A. Van Look et al., "Termination of Early Human Pregnancy with RU 486, *Human Reproduction,* vol. 4. no. 6, 1989, p. 718.

7. Author's interview with Dr. Lynette Nieman, December 13, 1989.

8. Author's private correspondence with Marc Bygdeman, March 29, 1990.

9. Chander P. Purl, Paul F. A. Van Look, eds. Symposium Proceedings, November 4, 1988, Bombay, India, P. 81.

10. "Induction of Labor," *Lancet,* 1985 2 (8642): 1019.

11. Author's interview with George Chrousos, Bethesda, Maryland, December 13, 1989.

12. Interview with Daniel Philibert, Paris, February 1, 1990; with Steven Grunberg by telephone, May 3, 1990.

13. Baulieu, "Steroid Receotors and Hormone Receptivity," *Journal of the American Medical Association,* August 15, 1976, vol. 125, part 2, p. 1049.

14. Marc Bygdeman et al., "Progesterone Receptor Blockage," *Contraception,* 32: 45, July 1985, No. 1.

15. Evin, *New York Times,* October 29, 1988, p. A1.

16. "Death drug", *New York Times,* October 28, 1988, p. A 34; "Pesticide:" *Christianity Today,* December 9, 1988, p. 16.

17. "Validity:" *New York Times,* March 16, 1990, p. A 35; Scheidler: *Church & State,* April 1985, p. 18; West: ACLU *Reproductive Rights,* February 16, 1990, p. 8.

18. California: Resolution 702-90, March 3-7, 1990; AMA: *New York Times,* June 29, 1990, p. A16.

19. Editorial, *Boston Globe,* January 14, 1990; editorial, *Washington Post,* February 17, 1990; editorial, *New York Times,* March 23, 1988, p. A 20.

20. Norton: *Los Angeles Times,* March 9, 1990, p. A 27; Mouttet: *New York Times,* July 29, 1990, p. A1.

9

Challenging the RU 486 Ban

In the early months of 1992, members of the ARM executive committee talked constantly on the phone and met in quick sessions. We were looking for a strategy of confrontation, patterned on that of Margaret Sanger, who knew that she risked arrest when she opened the first birth control clinic in 1916, but who also knew it was the only way to change an offensive law. We were looking for a strategy that would challenge President Bush and the Hoechst company directly, a way to dramatize the absurdity of their positions and bring the importance of RU 486 to the country and the media in vivid and simple terms.

Drawing on history, I suggested a legal attack based on Sanger's "One Package" case of 1936. She had arranged for a Japanese doctor to mail contraceptives to her medical director in New York, making sure that the government knew of it and that the package was seized. In the ensuing litigation, the U.S. Court of Appeals, 2nd Circuit, ruled that the customs law "was not designed to prevent importation of things which might intelligently be employed by conscientious and competent physicians to promote the well-being of patients." This decision brought a sizeable advance in the right of doctors to prescribe contraception, and we wondered if its broad language wasn't enough to encompass the mailing of RU 486.[1]

I had been in touch with a Chinese Research Institute that had made perfect copies of RU 486 for use on its patients. Now I convinced a Chinese scientist to bring some pills in his pocket, undeclared to U.S. Customs, when he visited the United States. We would check them for accuracy, and then attempt to persuade the Chinese Institute to mail a package of pills to a doctor in New York to start a test case. There were obstacles from Chinese officials, but our lawyers brought up more important problems. We had an impressive legal team: Marshall Beil, a constitutional expert who had handled our tax-exempt case against the Catholic church; Edward Costikyan, senior partner of a prominent New York firm, who had been a New York political leader; Milton Bass, a specialist in drug law; and Jesse Rothstein, whose expertise was in patents. Their conclusion was that "One Package" was now obsolete and applied only to contraception, not abortion. Instead, they suggested a new approach.

Why not have a pregnant American woman go to France or Britain and secure one dose of RU 486, which she would carry to New York to be administered by ARM's doctor? I would accompany her, carrying one dose of prostaglandin. The authorities here would be notified when the woman took the pills, setting up a test case.

France had to be eliminated after a week of phoning every clinic doctor that I knew. The Roussel company numbered every RU 486 pill, and doctors had to account for each one in writing. No doctor would take the risk of missing pills. In

Britain, RU 486 had been approved for public use in 1991, and I had close contact with a clinic director who agreed to give us one dose. The plan suddenly collapsed, however, when the British government imposed a ninety-day residency requirement similar to the long-standing one in France. This was a reversal of Britain's traditional policy of medical treatment for a citizen of any country, including treatment by vacuum abortion. It meant that an American woman could no longer be given RU 486 unless the clinic perjured itself about the ninety-day requirement, which was obviously impossible.

Studying the FDA laws intensely, our legal team came up with an even more meaningful strategy. RU 486 had been banned from the country under right-wing pressure, but in 1989 the FDA had adopted a "personal use" exemption to its banning powers that allowed a patient to bring a small amount of an unapproved drug into the country for dangerous illnesses such as Parkinson's disease. We would have no trouble finding a doctor to write a prescription. But the shaky point was whether a woman could argue that the trauma of an unwanted pregnancy met the "dangerous" requirement. Women's rights might thus become central to a lawsuit. Fortunately, we were able to secure Dr. Louise Tyrer for the project. She was a noted obstetrician-gynecologist, and had been vice president and medical director of Planned Parenthood Federation of America for many years until her retirement. Totally committed to breaking the ban against RU 486, she was willing to take a public stand and accept the risks.

Only Dr. Tyrer and I would know the source from which we secured one RU 486 dose. The lawyers explained the legal pitfalls. If the government ever brought Tyrer and me before a grand jury and gave us immunity, we would be legally bound to answer all questions. If we refused to name the source of RU 486, or any question, we could be sent to jail. To make certain no one else on the ARM board could be threatened, we set up a special organization to run the project, the ARM Research Council, Inc., with only myself and another officer involved. There began the exhausting search to find a clinic or doctor who would give us one dose of RU 486. In writing my book on RU 486 during the last few years, I had made scores of contacts, both overseas and in the United States. Now I sat on the phone day after day, begging and cajoling. Eventually I found the right scientist who was fascinated by the project and delivered some RU 486 to me.

The hardest step, unexpectedly, was to find a woman who would bring the test case. She had to be under nine weeks pregnant, under thirty-five years of age, a nonsmoker, a nondiabetic, with no history of hypertension. Above all, she had to be a dedicated feminist, courageous enough to undergo the rigors of the media and public exposure. We started with clinics we knew in New York and nearby states. We contacted women's "collectives" and campus groups. We visited clinics and interviewed their daily patient lists. One of the main hurdles was that most patients for vacuum abortion were taken at about nine weeks of pregnancy, and this was too late for RU 486. In a few weeks, our search had run to well over a hundred places and extended as far as Florida, Texas, and California.

There were severe disappointments along the way. One woman, with a Harvard degree, was a regular volunteer at a women's center and enthusiastic about our project. But after accepting, she called back a day later. She had a well-paid job

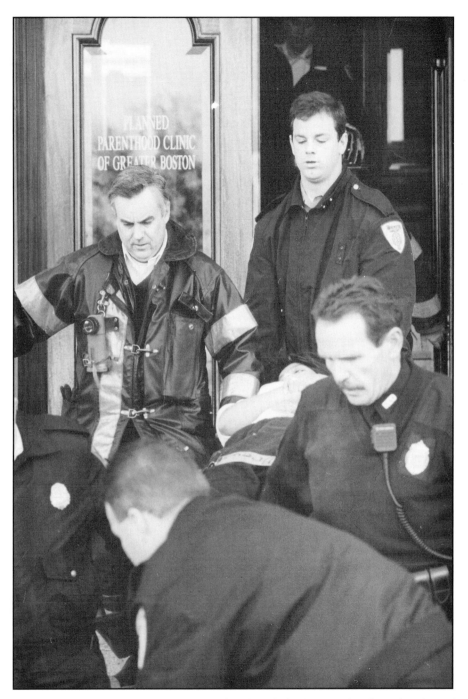

Emergency medical technicians move a shooting victim by stretcher from the Planned Parenthood clinic in Brookline, Massachusetts, Friday, December 30, 1994, after a gunman reportedly shot seven people in that clinic and in another abortion clinic nearby, killing two. (AP Worldwide Photo/Justin Ide)

In an attempt to repeal the federal comstock laws against birth control, Margaret Sanger testifies before a U.S. Senate Committee in 1931. Although her National Committee on federal legislation was backed by one thousand resolutions and more than twelve million signatures, the committee failed to convince Congress and closed down in 1937.

As a result of the tension between Sanger's time-consuming birth control campaign and her limited attention to her second husband Noah Slee, she promises in 1925 to "retire to the garden of love" with him if he donates $10,000 to a doctor who will run her clinics. Slee gave her the money, but she hardly decreased her schedule.

February 2, 1925

To Noah H. Slee,

1925 is to be the big year for the break in birth control.

If Dr. Cooper's association with us is successful I feel certain that the medical profession will take up the work. When the medical profession does this in the U.S.A. I shall feel that I have made my contribution to the cause & shall feel that I can withdraw from full time activity. I shall still want to publish the *Review* and take some interest in it & write articles & books in subjects allied with B.C. [Birth Control].

Sincerely Yours,

Margaret Sanger

Dr. Étienne-Émile Baulieu, a key scientist behind the development of RU 486, the French abortion pill, meets with Lawrence Lader at his apartment in New York in 1990.

In a dramatic challenge to the government's ban on the entry of RU 486 into the United States, Leona Benten, a pregnant woman carrying the pill, and Lawrence Lader, carrying a follow-up dose of prostaglandin, arrive in JFK airport on July 1, 1992. They are met by Dr. Louise Tyrer, Abortion Rights Mobilization medical doctor (left of Benten) and Eleanor Smeal, president of the Feminist Majority (right of Lader). U.S. Customs seized both drugs.

Escorts guarding a New York City Clinic in 1992. (Picture by Michael Culaso)

A Deputy State Fire Marshal tosses debris from inside the Brainerd, Minnesota, Planned Parenthood clinic, destroyed August 10, 1994, by an arson fire. The incident signaled an alarming trend of violence against reproductive health care providers that don't provide abortion care. The Brainerd Planned Parenthood clinic served the family planning needs of women in north central Minnesota for twenty-three years and did not offer abortion services. Despite numerous leads and an extensive federal, state, and local investigation, no one has been charged with setting this fire.

Rosie Jimenez (1950–1977), a single mother, with a five-year–old daughter, was a scholarship student six months away from receiving her teaching credentials. She was the first known victim of the Hyde Amendment, which blocked funding of abortion for medicaid patients. Too poor to pay for an abortion in a private clinic, she died in agony from septicemia after an illegal abortion. Today, only thirteen states provide medicaid funding for abortions.

Large numbers show their support in April 5, 1992 March for Women's Lives in Washington, D.C. (Photo courtesy of National Organization for Women)

In a dramatic challenge to the government's ban on the entry of RU 486 into the United States, Leona Benten, a pregnant woman carrying the pill, and Lawrence Lader, carrying a follow-up dose of prostaglandin, arrive in JFK airport on July 1, 1992. They are met by Dr. Louise Tyrer, Abortion Rights Mobilization medical doctor (left of Benten) and Eleanor Smeal, president of the Feminist Majority (right of Lader). U.S. Customs seized both drugs.

Escorts guarding a New York City Clinic in 1992. (Picture by Michael Culaso)

A Deputy State Fire Marshal tosses debris from inside the Brainerd, Minnesota, Planned Parenthood clinic, destroyed August 10, 1994, by an arson fire. The incident signaled an alarming trend of violence against reproductive health care providers that don't provide abortion care. The Brainerd Planned Parenthood clinic served the family planning needs of women in north central Minnesota for twenty-three years and did not offer abortion services. Despite numerous leads and an extensive federal, state, and local investigation, no one has been charged with setting this fire.

Rosie Jimenez (1950–1977), a single mother, with a five-year–old daughter, was a scholarship student six months away from receiving her teaching credentials. She was the first known victim of the Hyde Amendment, which blocked funding of abortion for medicaid patients. Too poor to pay for an abortion in a private clinic, she died in agony from septicemia after an illegal abortion. Today, only thirteen states provide medicaid funding for abortions.

Large numbers show their support in April 5, 1992 March for Women's Lives in Washington, D.C. (Photo courtesy of National Organization for Women)

and worried that her employer would see her picture in the papers or see her on television. She felt she had to place her work ahead of her commitment to the women's movement. Another candidate, who accepted at first, became increasingly concerned about the legal implications. If she were called before a grand jury, could she be indicted? We assured her that no woman had ever been convicted of abortion since the first anti-abortion laws were passed before the Civil War. We had our lawyers spend considerable time reassuring her on the phone, and even gave her a written guarantee that we would supply free legal defense if needed. Finally, she admitted she was in the middle of a divorce, and feared that any publicity on RU 486 could damage the proceedings. "Everything's closing in on me," she complained before pulling out.

A third candidate seemed ideal, absolutely determined to have an RU 486 abortion. She had read my book and knew all about RU 486. Dr. Tyrer spoke with her on the phone and was equally impressed. The woman held a low-level position at an international trading company, and insisted that her boss supported abortion rights and that she had no worry about losing her job. As a final check, we invited her to dinner to meet a few members of the executive committee. She arrived with an older man whom I quickly assumed was her boss and probably responsible for the pregnancy.

The meeting turned out to be a soap opera fiasco. When I went over the scenario of flying to London and returning to JFK airport in New York to meet the press, the woman's friend grew anguished.

"But I explained all this to you," she told him.

"No, darling. Impossible!" he cried. "My wife, a jealous Italian. You appear at a press conference, and my wife, the office, everyone will know about us. All I've worked for will be swept away in one big wave."

She insisted their affair would be kept secret. "I'm determined to go through with it," she argued.

"You do this and I don't talk to you," he shouted.

"You try to stop me, and I won't talk to you," she countered.

When they left, the executive committee members quickly decided she was the wrong candidate.

We had almost lost hope that we would find someone when I telephoned Steve Heilig, an executive of the San Francisco Medical Society, who had extensive clinic contacts in the area. He called back a few days later with the name of Leona Benten. She was twenty-nine, a social worker who had just lost her job, obviating the problem of employment pressure. She was a committed feminist and highly intelligent with the stability to stand up under media attention. After Dr. Tyrer and I had long talks with her on the phone, we decided to gamble the airfare and bring her immediately to New York. Leona arrived at our apartment on Sunday, June 28, and Dr. Tyrer flew in from Nevada. We were all entranced with Leona's wit, soundness, and commitment. She had arrived with only two pairs of blue jeans and we suggested that a more formal attire might be better for the airport press conference. My wife dug up a black skirt that turned out to be a perfect fit.

Meanwhile, there was a frantic day of booking air tickets,

writing press releases, and rehearsing our volunteer staff in sending faxes to the media and sending notification of our challenge of the law to the FDA and to U.S. Customs. Since all faxes had to be sent between 9 and 11 A.M. the morning of our arrival, every detail had to mesh flawlessly.

Leona and I boarded our plane Monday evening and arrived early the next morning. When British customs questioned the brevity of our stay, I said we were attending family planning meetings. With a quick stop at the museums, I added with a smile. I taxied Leona to her hotel, went myself to a Pall Mall club, where rates were modest, made a quick stop at the National Gallery, and took Leona for lunch at a classic London pub.

I was in a deep sleep at the club in late afternoon when my wife phoned from New York. The executive committee had decided the faxes were too numerous and complicated to send within two hours the next morning, and wanted permission to send them now. There was a risk that a journalist might leak the story to the London authorities, and we could be detained. But the gamble had to be taken.

On the plane to New York on July 1, we worked over Leona's statement to the press. Slightly nauseated, she slept a good deal. An hour before arrival, I gave her an envelope with one dose of pills and kept the prostaglandin dose myself. She went to the bathroom to change into her skirt. When we presented our passports on disembarking, there was a sheet of paper on the official's desk with both our names written largely. We were asked at customs if we carried unapproved drugs, and we said we did. Leona was taken to a private room where they refused to let me accompany her. I told them our lawyer was outside the gate and had the right to be present, but they denied the request. Leona told me later she had given them the pills, but she and her luggage were still searched. I went through the same procedure when I handed over the prostaglandin.

Although I knew our volunteers had been on the phones with the media all morning, and that we had crafted a challenge to the admission of RU 486 that would appeal to the press, I thought at best we might be met by a dozen reporters. Instead, when we walked through the customs gate with Leona's striped, African-style cap perched jauntily on her head, the mob of television cameras and reporters staggered us. Our staff later made a count of at least forty-five.

Dr. Tyrer, modishly dressed, rushed forward to embrace us. In my statement to the press, I stressed the legal basis of our challenge. Dr. Tyrer spoke on RU 486's benefits to women and particularly its use for more cancer research. Leona spoke movingly about why her doctors considered RU 486 better for her than a vacuum abortion. When she described how customs had seized her pills, she wiped the tears from her eyes and cupped her chin in her hands, making a striking picture that would appear constantly in newspapers and on television.

That evening every TV network and most local stations carried the story. The *New York Times,* the *Washington Post,* and many major papers gave us prominent space. We were flooded with interview requests, and I even got up at 5:30 the next morning to do an early show. We had accomplished our mission of focusing national attention on RU 486, and at the same time putting pressure on the government and Hoechst-Roussel to start the long process of bringing the pill to American women.

Now our legal team worked to prepare the court papers that would retrieve the RU 486 pills for Leona before their effectiveness [the ninth week of pregnancy] ran out. Marshall Beil had been ARM's lawyer for many years, but he lacked the staff for a concentrated effort. The Center for Reproductive Law and Policy, which had just split off from the ACLU, phoned me and offered their *pro bono* services. We agreed to have them work with Beil. The legal team submitted soundly researched legal papers to the federal district court in Brooklyn. The hearing date was set for July 10, before Judge Charles Sifton. He had been appointed by President Carter so we felt we were likely to get a fair chance. Still, I was nervous when I took an early subway to Brooklyn and entered the austere, wood-paneled courtroom. Simon Heller of the center argued that the FDA regulations covered importation of an unapproved drug for personal use, that the ban terming RU 486 "dangerous" was backed by no scientific evidence, and that the FDA had not asked for public testimony as was required by administrative law.

Government lawyers insisted that the personal-use exemption applied only to illnesses like Parkinson's and AIDS. They were thus establishing two classes of patients, placing women and any trauma of pregnancy in an inferior category.

Judge Sifton set July 14 at 10 A.M. for his decision. We reassembled in court that morning, hardly expecting how strongly he would support our position. "This was a lawsuit waiting to happen," Sifton announced. Labeling the FDA's actions a "history of political and bureaucratic timidity," and a "sink of illegality," he concluded that "she is right that the FDA has proceeded illegally" and ordered the RU 486 pills returned to Leona immediately.[2]

I hugged Leona. Everything we had worked for had turned into a dazzling reality. A car was waiting downstairs, and Dr. Tyrer and Leona drove off to JFK to retrieve the pills.

Meanwhile, the government's lawyers had adopted a shocking, duplicitous strategy. They claimed they had phoned customs, but no release order for the pills came through. Other government lawyers rushed to the U.S. Court of Appeals, 2nd Circuit, with a request, obviously prepared ahead of time, to stay Sifton's order. The court granted it, leaving Tyrer and Leona waiting purposelessly at JFK. ARM's legal team tried to resolve the impasse by asking for a three-judge panel of the circuit to meet at 4 P.M.

The panel could not have been more harmful to our cause. It was made up of John Walker, President Bush's first cousin; J. Daniel Mahoney, former chair of the New York State Conservative Party, which was strongly antiabortion; and Frank Altimari, a Reagan appointee. Their questions from the bench quickly showed their prejudices. One judge even asked why Leona had to carry RU 486 into New York to produce an abortion when she could have just as well taken the pills on the plane (despite her nausea and exhaustion, and the danger that no doctor was in attendance). It was hardly unexpected that the panel agreed to a stay, and decided that the pills should not be returned to Leona. Our resounding triumph in Judge Sifton's court had been snatched from us.

Media coverage intensified as the case neared its climax. The press was entranced by the spectacle of one frail woman in a battle with the government over the simple issue of securing the abortion of her choice. Leona was hounded with requests for interviews. In fact, she was so exhausted that one night she turned down two networks.

To repossess the pills for Leona, our sole legal recourse was the U.S. Supreme Court. We had to go through Justice Clarence Thomas, hardly sympathetic to abortion rights, who was assigned to this circuit. "We want to strike down a symbol of the Bush administration's efforts to block access to abortion," declared our lawyer from the Center for Reproductive Law and Policy. The Supreme Court accepted the appeal. On July 18, just seventeen days after we had landed at JFK with RU 486, the Court avoided any ruling on the constitutional issues involved,[3] but by a seven-to-two vote refused to return the pills to Leona. "They bowed to political pressure," Leona announced. "This ban denies my rights as a woman for equal protection under the law, my right of privacy and other constitutional guarantees."[4] Now Leona had no other recourse but vacuum abortion to solve her unwanted pregnancy.

The case had been a legal gamble from the start, of course, but it had turned out far more successfully than anyone expected. Leona personally had lost, but the movement had made a striking advance in bringing the issue of RU 486 to national attention and shaking up the government's rigidity in the process. ARM had no intention of resting on its gains. Our skill was in finding the right strategies. We now had to develop new strategies to intensify the pressure on Hoechst-Roussel and the government. We quickly decided that the most daring and productive move was to make an exact copy of RU 486 in our own laboratory in the United States, and prove that the pill was no longer a Roussel monopoly and could be easily reproduced for widespread distribution here. That objective would consume us for the next year.

10

Making an American Abortion Pill

The election of Bill Clinton to the presidency in November 1992 totally reversed the political climate for RU 486. Not only had he campaigned on an abortion rights platform, with the women's movement a major factor in his support, but he advocated the immediate entry of the pill into the United States. On January 22, 1993, the twentieth anniversary of the *Roe* v. *Wade* decision, he instructed Secretary of Health and Human Services Donna Shalala to "promote the testing, licensing and manufacturing in the United States of RU 486 or other antiprogestins."[1]

With repeated firebombings of abortion clinics increasing the need for the privacy advantage of RU 486, our pressure would be concentrated solely on the Hoechst-Roussel company. We decided to try a Chinese approach. Roussel was nervous about China. Ignoring international patents, the Chinese government had made a proved copy of the pill and already tested it on at least ten thousand women.

If we bought an ample supply of Chinese pills, we could threaten Roussel with the possibility of breaking its monopoly. By testing our own version of the pill here, we could prove to

Roussel that we had competitive American scientists and that we refused to be stalled any longer by Roussel's blockade of American interests.

American friends of mine, working in China and well-connected with its medical community, started exploring at my request the agencies responsible for the Chinese pill. Soon I heard from a Chinese doctor at Peking Union Medical College, who was director of the country's RU 486 program. She gave us permission to buy pills from her and test them here under an approved protocol. She also would supply us with the Chinese studies on the making and testing of their pill that would prove invaluable to our scientists when we started to make our own copy.

Because my American friends were coming back to the United States shortly on vacation, I sent them the money to buy the pills, and they brought them through customs without declaring them and with no check of their baggage. We already had a small supply of French RU 486 on hand from the extra doses secured for the Leona Benten project. Our scientists were thus able to run two tests at different university labs to compare the French pill with the Chinese copy.

An organic chemistry analysis showed that the active chemical ingredients in both pills were indistinguishable. A blood profile study in primates to compare the pharmacologic and metabolic character of both pills gave us further corroboration that they were effectively the same.

In a press conference in New York on February 17, 1993, heavily attended by the networks and print media, I announced that, "We expect our testing will prove to the Roussel company that it can no longer deny American women one of the most efficient and safest methods of early abortion. We will accept no more evasions or delays." We never did start testing the Chinese pill on women since our contacts at the FDA implied that they would have a lot more faith in our own copy of the pill than the Chinese version. Still, the Chinese pills and Chinese technical papers enabled our scientists to break down and study the chemical components of the pill when beginning work in our own laboratory. The strategy of importing the Chinese version also seemed to make an impact on Roussel.

Just a week after our press conference, Dr. Eduard Sakiz, president of Roussel, came to Washington, D.C., to meet with Dr. David Kessler, head of the FDA. He announced that the drug should be made available in the United States. It was a significant step, described in a *New York Times* headline, "DOOR MAY BE OPEN FOR ABORTION PILL TO BE SOLD IN U.S." A *Times* editorial reported, "Still fearing a boycott, the company does not want to get directly involved in distributing the drug."[2] It was increasingly important that we start making our own pill.

The search for a skilled scientist, who knew the antiprogestin field, including RU 486, took many months. I went to Dr. M. C. Chang of the Worcester Foundation for Experimental Biology, an old associate who had been codeveloper of the birth control pill along with Dr. Pincus. He supplied me with a potential list. Other friends at university chemistry departments gave me names. All were tied up with teaching or long-range research projects. Columbia University finally became the key. The department chair had gone to the same school as I had. A relative of mine was a heavy donor. Analyzing those who had taken Ph.D. degrees there, Columbia came up with a scientist from a somewhat distant state.

His credentials were excellent. Fortunately, he could take leave from his research institute. But the problem was money. He not only asked a high salary, but since he lived a thousand miles away, we had to cover his living expenses here as well as frequent travel home for himself and his family. A second problem was anonymity. Because he did not want his employer to know this connection, and wanted the same protection at our lab from antiabortion attacks, he would only be known as Dr. X. By the time our lawyer (the only other one to know his name) had drawn up a contract, we were committed to heavy spending.

Finding a supervising scientist who would check the weekly progress and final results was easier. The Columbia Chemistry Department had a brilliant young scientist, Dr. David Horne, who was not only an expert in antiprogestins but fascinated by the project. He soon became an essential member of our team.

To maintain total secrecy, the project would be run by the ARM Research Council, and all bills, checks, and mail covered by that name alone. If we were ever forced to put some label on our work, it would be called cancer research, which was not too far off the mark since it was hoped that RU 486 would prove advantageous in cancer treatment as well.

Raising the money, which would come to hundreds of thousands of dollars, became a laborious task. The main donor was a Midwest foundation, which had helped the abortion rights campaign from its earliest days, but preferred anonymity. Other long-time supporters, like Phil Harvey of Washington, D.C., were equally generous. When our reserves ran low in the last months, I was begging for checks of $1,000.

The search for a laboratory where the pill would be made

produced the same frustrations. Because Mayor David Dinkins had been an outspoken advocate of RU 486, it seemed logical that an empty lab in the New York City university system would be an easy answer. We found two such labs available for rental, but we could never surmount the clearance process of the academic bureaucracy. Private universities had the same problems. Our project, although vaguely identified, smelled of controversy. Educators invariably fled from controversy, fearing that if any Catholic official got a clue of the abortion connection, alumni donations from Catholics and conservatives could be quickly diminished.

After months were frittered away, we decided that the only solution was to build our own lab. This, too, assumed the trappings of a CIA operation. We had to have a "cover," and I found it eventually through an old friend who had rented space in a warehouse in a Westchester, New York, suburb, where he intended to produce a new product. Because his plans were delayed, he rented the space to us, telling the owner of the property we were part of his operation.

For months, however, everything went wrong. An extra large hood, required to vent fumes, became highly expensive and difficult to position so that it could vent through the only convenient opening in the roof. Cabinets and sinks had to be designed for an unfortunately small space. We bought testing equipment, but the most sophisticated of all was priced so high that the scientists had to work out an arrangement with a local university to use their facilities once or twice a week. Building and electrical inspectors gave us further headaches. Before getting a license, we had to install, or rewire, fire prevention devices. Special garbage collections had to be worked out to remove chemical residues. A constant supply of dry ice was essential, and the scientists had to make frequent trips to the nearest supplier, which was fifteen miles away.

Since at that point we were still considering testing our pill under New York's "Mini-FDA" law, which allowed a new drug to be cleared by state authorities rather than the federal FDA, every ingredient in the pill had to be bought within the boundaries of New York. This was no easy matter. It often meant that our scientists had to search for days on the phone, trying to find the manufacturer of some obscure chemical whose billing would be from a New York address.

We had hoped to produce 50 grams of RU 486 (a relatively small amount) in six months. But it was soon obvious we couldn't meet the deadline. The main obstacle was the small size of our lab and the limitations of our equipment.

Each step of the ten-step synthesis had to be repeated many times because the equipment could only hold limited ingredients. Each step was carefully recorded in the daily log book and checked by instruments to be sure the results were accurate. Dr. Horne would come to the lab to approve the work. Sometimes one batch was slightly different than another. Sometimes the work had to be redone.

When the 50 grams were finally completed in late March 1993, we were at a strategic crossroads. Our RU 486 was only enough to supply abortions to about a hundred women. There was no patent problem with Roussel since our lawyers informed us that under the law [35 U.S. Code 271 (e) (1)], research was permissible as long as the pills weren't sold to women. Testing this small a number would essentially be symbolic, but it would prove to the country that RU 486 could be made here, and a lot more of the drug would be available shortly thereafter.

This was a time of multiple strategies. We had to pressure Roussel from many directions. One of our lawyers had previously cited a federal law that might allow us to weaken, or even eliminate, Roussel's grip on the RU 486 patent, and a New York University law student had researched 28 U.S. Code 1498 exhaustively. Patent removals were rare, and most occurred during emergency situations in both world wars. But there were a few nonmilitary precedents where the U.S. government had appropriated a patent for the public interest—a water irradiation patent in Milwaukee, for example, that would benefit public health—and our lawyers felt this approach could be kept as a threat to Roussel although its chances of success were skimpy.

Our original strategy, first outlined in my book on RU 486 in 1991, had been to test our copy of the pill under the New York State "Mini-FDA" law. The advantages to us were essentially political. With both Gov. Mario Cuomo and Attorney General Robert Abrams being long-time adherents of abortion rights, we felt our chances of clearing the bureaucracy were a lot better than going through the federal FDA.

Marshall Beil, our lawyer, wrote Abrams, defining the scope of Education Law 6817, which covered drug testing, and we met with his legal staff.[3] Our aim was to get a few supporters in the legislature to ask the attorney general for a legal opinion, thus expediting our testing application. But after Abrams resigned to seek higher office, this approach was weakened. Beil then wrote to the chair of the New York State Board of Pharmacy, which controlled new drug testing, asking for an immediate appointment. This request must have stunned the board, which had probably never handled a new drug application, and was made up, we found later, of highly conservative and unsophisticated members.

After a long delay, the board wrote back, first asking us to prove that the "FDA has no authority in this matter," and second stating that "no funds are available in our current budget to undertake such an elaborate process."[4]

We replied that when the statute had been amended in 1969, its legislative sponsor had intended to give it, according to his statement, "Jurisdiction over intrastate drug operations ... comparable in scope to the Federal requirements." As to the second point, we told the board that ARM was willing to cover the cost of testing.

To harness a unified front of the legislature behind our application, we then called a meeting of key members of the State Assembly including Helene Weinstein and Richard Gottfried. They decided to draft a resolution, to be signed by a majority of the Assembly, demanding the Pharmacy Board's compliance with the law. Working behind the scenes, we also contacted a majority of the sixteen members of the Board of Regents, which controlled the Pharmacy Board.

At that point, we learned from our Washington contacts that the FDA might give serious consideration to approving the testing of our pill. Edward Costikyan, one of our lawyers and an old friend of Secretary of Health and Human Services Donna Shalala, put the question to her bluntly. Despite Roussel's meeting with the FDA, Secretary Shalala wrote back: "These actions do not, of course, preclude your clients from pursuing the study and approval of their version of RU 486."[5]

We now had the federal as well as the New York State route open to us, and immediately set up an appointment with FDA officials.

Now it was time for the ultimate pressure on Roussel: the announcement that we had made our own copy of the abortion pill so secretly that extremists had never been able to sabotage us. At a heavily attended press conference on April 1, 1993, we showed the pill to reporters. Photographers and TV cameras seized on the dramatic shot of the aspirin-sized object lying in my somewhat sweaty palm. "Our purpose is to pressure Roussel," I announced. "We are trying to get them into immediate and decisive action." The FDA would be discussing testing with us shortly. If Roussel kept delaying, we would urge the government to seize its patent. I read from a letter I had written Secretary Shalala: "Under 28 U.S.C. 1498, your Department can contract with a drug company in this country or elsewhere to manufacture and distribute RU 486 to American women at cost."

U.S. Rep. Ron Wyden (D-Oregon), who headed the House subcommittee on small business, took up our theme. At a press conference in Washington the next day, he threatened to strip Roussel "of the U.S. patent on RU 486 if it does not take steps to make the drug available." The American Medical Association and other medical associations demanded that Roussel "have the drug formally presented [to the FDA] for investigative and research purposes."[6]

Meanwhile, Dr. Horne kept most of our copy of RU 486 at his laboratory at Columbia University. For safety, I kept some of it at my house. In an article on me on October 18, 1993, the *New Yorker* magazine seemed amused by this quaint storage and reported that "in his refrigerator there he keeps a plastic jar that is two-thirds full of white powder. . . . The jar in Lader's fridge holds part of the group's stash of the drug."

From our Washington contacts, we learned of a new crisis. There was a mounting campaign, undoubtedly organized by antiabortion groups, to force the Monsanto company to remove its product Cytotec from the market. Cytotec was a prostaglandin, widely used in the treatment of ulcers, but also essential as a followup dose to intensify the action of the abortion pill. Its unavailability would damage American women. They would have to resort to an inferior product. To counter this threat, I secured a list of Monsanto board members, and tried to pinpoint a few who might have prochoice leanings from their biographies in *Who's Who*. Then I wrote to Joan T. Bok, chair of the New England Electric system, and Dr. Philip Leder, a Harvard Medical School professor, among others. When we received virtually similar letters assuring that Monsanto "has no intention of removing Cytotec from the market,"[7] we felt the danger had been averted.

The first meaningful breakthrough from Roussel came on April 20, 1993, when Dr. Kessler, head of the FDA, announced that the French company had made a verbal agreement with the Population Council of New York, a prominent research institute developing family planning techniques.

Roussel would supply two thousand pills and all its research data on the pill's development. The Population Council would test about two thousand women nationwide, and be responsible for finding a company to manufacture and distribute RU 486 after approval by the FDA.

No contract had been signed. Yet Dr. Kessler optimistically

predicted RU 486 could be approved in four to six months as a result of the backup data from Roussel. One of our contacts estimated that it would take two years for approval; another estimated four years. In my memo to the ARM board, I wrote: "Our aim must be to shorten this time radically."

On April 27, ARM sent a letter to the Population Council offering its full cooperation. We cited our assets. We had produced 50 grams of RU 486 in our laboratory. Our scientists knew exactly how to make the pill, and therefore they could speed up the work of any manufacturer selected. Dr. Louise Tyrer, our medical director, could help organize the testing of volunteers. A business group we knew was investigating potential manufacturers. We had the backing of the women's movement, which could make available feminist clinics as testing sites.

On May 4, we met with a panel of FDA scientists. Our group included Dr. Horne, Dr. Tyrer and myself. It was an unspoken assumption that the Population Council's negotiations could drag on endlessly. Therefore, the FDA was receptive to immediate testing of our copy of the pill. Rather than go through the long process of securing our own Investigative New Drug (IND) approval, the FDA suggested we might be able to cross-reference under the Population Council's existent IND, which had been in force since a few experimental tests at the University of California at Los Angeles and elsewhere in 1983.

On May 10, 1993, Dr. Tyrer, Faye Wattleton, former president of Planned Parenthood Federation, and I met with Dr. Rosemarie Thau of the Population Council. She wrote us shortly afterward: "I am pleased to tell you that for its part, the

Population Council has no objections to your cross-referencing to the IND."[8] The problem was that since the research data for the IND came from Roussel, we would also have to have Roussel's permission.

It was obvious that Roussel was inflicting a long wait on both the Population Council and ARM. The tension grew with each week.

NOTES

1. "Memo for the Secretary of Health & Human Services" from The White House, Office of the Press Secretary.

2. *New York Times,* February 3, 1993, p. A 1.

3. Education Law, Title VIII, The Professions, Article 137, Pharmacy, NY, CLS, Education 6817 (1990).

4. Letter of October 18, 1983, from Lawrence H. Mokhiber, executive secretary, State Board of Pharmacy, to Marshall Beil, ARM's lawyer.

5. Letter of November 7, 1993, from Secretary of Health and Human Services Donna E. Shalala to Edward N. Costikyan, ARM's lawyer.

6. American Political Network Abortion Report, April 2, 1993, p. 2. Headline: RU 486.

7. Letters of Leder, April 7, 1993, and of Bok, April 26, 1993, to author.

8. Letter of July 8, 1993, from Thau to author.

11

A Dangerous Game: Delaying the Pill

It was a bad year, a painful year of evasions and even deceit. After the Hoechst-Roussel company announced in 1993 it was negotiating with the Population Council to turn over the patent for RU 486, U.S. Rep. Ron Wyden optimistically predicted "clinical trials in the next three or four months." André Ulmann, a Roussel executive, estimated "nine to fifteen months for clinical tests and approval [by the FDA]." It was all vaporous talk. Nothing really happened.

Hoechst kept issuing alarming threats. One month they were asking to be indemnified for any loss of business in the United States. Another month they insisted they couldn't contract with the Population Council unless a major manufacturer was found. What constituted major: giants like Merck or American Home Products? Obviously, companies of that size, with hundreds of products, would not take on an abortion pill for fear of being picketed and losing business. It was logical to assume that Hoechst was indulging in another evasive tactic.

Abortion Rights Mobilization was in a peculiar bind. We were convinced we had to start testing two to three thousand women immediately with our copy of RU 486, but we didn't know if the FDA would clear us while the Population Council negotiations were going on. On May 4, 1993, we met with an FDA panel of eight scientists and our doubts were resolved. Dr. Horne gave them all his research data, and his tests proving our copy was equivalent to RU 486. I stressed we had to begin testing in less than a year. It was like a "family meeting," one scientist confided later, concluding that the Hoechst negotiations were a "sham."

On May 10, I wrote Margaret Catley-Carson, president of the Population Council, reporting on our FDA meeting and pledging our full cooperation in any united action. The Population Council held large planning meetings in May and June. They announced there would be "several 'tiers' of advisory groups." They were worried about money, insisting that the early stage of trials would cost $4 million, a figure far above our estimates. In a July memo, they wrote:

> While the large conglomerate and pharmaceutical manufacturers have not to date shown interest in manufacturing RU 486, there has been good interest in the project from medium and small-size companies.

The danger of a black market had been ignored, but a fanciful entrepreneur in Florida sent ARM an ad he was about to place in newspapers. For a $19.90 postal order, Women's Information Services would supply the "quickest, easiest, most comfortable and least expensive way for you to get RU 486."

The entrepreneur was setting up a clinic with a supervising doctor on an island near Florida whose authorities, he claimed, had guaranteed he would be immune from U.S. law. Twice a week or more, depending on the demand, he would fly women from Florida to the island, obviously making considerable money from the chartered flights as well as the cost to the woman for the pill. Since ARM was the only organization that had made an exact copy of RU 486, where was he getting his pills? He had a relative, he confided, who worked at Hoechst headquarters and could ship him a steady supply. ARM refused the man's advances, and nothing was heard from him again.

While the Population Council was spending mouths examining a long list of small manufacturers, we at ARM were convinced we could find the right plant quickly. We surveyed a dozen in the United States from New Jersey to California. It was easy to get their financial statements. On the phone, I could gauge the commitment of the president and the company's experience with antiprogestins. Only a Philadelphia plant seemed logical, and when they began to worry about security measures, ARM came to the conclusion that any U.S. plant could be picketed, or even firebombed, and that the only solution was to manufacture overseas.

The best source was a prestigious scientist at the National Institutes of Health, a long-time adviser, who immediately suggested three European manufacturers. I phoned them, and they faxed back scientific and financial summaries. Dr. Horne and I agreed on the British prospect. Its president had a string of impressive degrees. He had taught for years at two universities before setting up his laboratory. He sent us pictures of it. He described clients with whom he had worked in clearing products through the FDA. He gave us a synopsis of his approach to the synthesis of RU 486. Fortunately, he was coming to New

York in about a week. Dr. Horne and I met him in a quiet nook of a congenial club, and we talked almost all afternoon. I have watched Dr. Horne's reaction to many scientists. I had never seen him so impressed by one before.

The British plant faxed us a draft of their contract, its costs, which seemed fair, and a description of how they would work through the synthesis and set up analytic standards. Although they would do all the lab work, they had a partner nearby that was skilled in mass production, and would take over the final production of three thousand doses for us. On April 20, 1994, we signed a contract.

There was a problem of finding large amounts of estradiol, the basic ingredient of RU 486, made by only a few labs. We also had to find an insurance company that would cover our British plant.

To run the tests that would get our product through the FDA, we decided to test at a prominent laboratory in Virginia.

The first part would be toxicology on rats and dogs with some doses a hundred times greater than that given to women to prove that no ingredient in our pill could be dangerous. The second part was "bioequivalency" studies on rats and rabbits to show that our pill's action on reproduction and other functions was equivalent to that of the French RU 486. Our protocol for testing was then submitted to the FDA.

The ongoing hurdle was that Hoechst kept insisting that its negotiations were serious. Investment groups that wanted to produce and market RU 486 wrote ARM. We interviewed the most likely candidates. Dr. George Brown of the Population Council told me that his organization had set Thanksgiving 1993 as a final deadline. The date passed, and talks went on.

In February 1994, the Marie Stopes clinic in London announced it would accept American women and other nonresidents for RU 486. The advantages were minuscule. The clinic's fee was $500, and American women would have to pay the airfare to London as well as a week's hotel and food while they waited for followup care. Few women could afford the total package.

In March I decided to make the ultimate challenge to Hoechst: an op-ed piece in the *New York Times*. It boldly announced ARM's testing plan and predicted "as early as the end of the year, the pill could be made available to women to participate in field tests." Citing the law that allowed a patent to be removed if the public interest is at stake, I urged that, "Congress should begin holding hearings on this possibility immediately."[1]

Only the president of Hoechst will ever know what factors swayed him after a year of seemingly fruitless talk. I suspect President Clinton used some sort of economic prod. On April 14, Secretary Shalala and Dr. Kessler met with Roussel officers in Washington and supposedly gave them a May 15 deadline. Congressman Wyden, echoing my op-ed piece, threatened to start hearings on patent removal. I am not downplaying the impact of ARM's four-pronged strategy: the challenge to the customs ban, the importation of Chinese pills, the making of our own exact copy of RU 486, and finally the international influence of a *Times* article. Still, the government's role seems critical. Secretary Shalala knew how to use White House pressure.

On May 16, 1994, came an epochal announcement. The Hoechst-Roussel company had signed a contract with the Pop-

ulation Council, turning over its American RU 486 patent without charge, as well as all research data and studies that had gone
into the making of the pill. The Population Council announced
that it would conduct trials on two thousand women, using
French pills that would be turned over to it. After that, the council would have to manufacture its own pills for mass distribution
in the United States. "The FDA will do all it can to quickly eval-
uate mifepristone (RU 486)," Secretary Shalala promised.[2]

The contract was a tremendous gain for American women,
and a tribute to the council's persistence in long negotiations.
ARM was now in a nebulous position. What could we offer the
council to speed up the FDA approval process? First, in Dr.
Horne we had the only scientist who had made an exact copy
of the pill and knew every nuance in this difficult synthesis.
Second, we had a prestigious British plant that could manufacture the pill at a fair price. The plant had already spent six
weeks in the first steps of synthesis. We ordered them to stop,
but to keep all materials and records we had already paid for.

I offered to put these two advantages at the service of the
Population Council and asked for an appointment with President Catley-Carson. In our June 24 meeting, I pointed out that
the council's talks with two major pharmaceutical companies
here could lead to inflated prices. Norplant, which had been
developed by the council, offered a precedent. The American
manufacturer had put the price far beyond the means of many
women. Our British plant could not only keep prices lower, but
could ensure security in a country that refused to tolerate
antiabortion furor. Any manufacturing must be done overseas.

I also suggested an efficient way to cut the cost of distribution and marketing here. Why pay a company for a needless

service? By setting up a one-person office in Britain, a hospital, clinic, or doctor could fax that office a request for any number of doses of RU 486, which would be immediately packaged and sent by overnight service.

Such a plan would also eliminate the danger of attacks on a U.S. distributor. Catley-Carson listened politely. But although I stressed the importance of getting RU 486 to American women quickly, I got the impression that the council would spend an inordinate amount of time interviewing potential manufacturers and money sources. At least I convinced the council to consider our British plant, and they signed a mutual secrecy agreement in July. ARM then turned over to the council all its documents and contracts from the plant. It was a gamble, but I wanted to prove how highly we rated the British.

On a European swing in early September, I inspected the British plant in person, and was impressed by its building, laboratories, and staff. In Paris, I met with Dr. Étienne Baulieu and Dr. André Ulmann, a Roussel executive. They told me that Dr. David Grimes at San Francisco General Hospital would be conducting a World Health Organization study on the use of RU 486 as a "morning after" pill, the only U.S. site among fourteen countries.

Drs. Baulieu and Ulmann stressed the huge cost of bringing RU 486 to the American market, and suggested I talk to a financial group in Washington, D.C. They felt this group was interested in women's rights, not just profits. After talking with the group's president, I agreed.

Now we had an advantageous package to offer the Population Council: a combination of ARM's scientists, the British plant, and the Washington group's financing. I called Margaret

Catley-Carson to make an appointment, purposefully after election day, and we set on November 15. The election results of November 8 were a disaster for abortion rights. Antichoice legislators won a majority of the House. The issue was still unclear in the Senate. Congress was under Republican control for the first time since 1952. RU 486 was in particular danger. With the House Judiciary Committee chaired by Henry Hyde (R-Illinois), vehemently anti-abortion, and most key committees chaired by similar extremists, a bill to ban RU 486 in the United States could be introduced in 1995. Even if Clinton vetoed it, there was no certainty that prochoice members could gain a third of the votes in either chamber to uphold a veto. And there was no certainty of a prochoice president after 1996.

Our board now believed the political crisis completely dominated RU 486's prospects. It was critical to get the pill distributed to women nationwide before the end of 1995 so that it would become imbedded in society's consciousness and be difficult to eliminate. I hammered hard at our conclusions in my meeting with Margaret Catley-Carson, but was dismayed to find her schedule didn't call for national distribution until August 1996, almost a year after our deadline.

The Population Council had started its trials using two thousand French pills, but it still had not decided on a manufacturer or money source. I pushed vigorously for the British plant and the Washington group, stressing that production of the American pill could start immediately if the council would accept our package, including a coalition of ARM, NOW, Feminist Majority, and other groups to handle lobbying, public education, and public relations, our expertise. I told Catley-Carson that we knew she was negotiating with a manufacturer that we considered a bad choice. It was located in a small country without the scientific record of Britain nor the essential political stability and financial reserves that Britain offered. I asked if she could make a decision on the British plant in a week or two, but she felt that was too short a time. It was obvious that the Population Council would keep moving at a slow pace.

ARM now had to make a hard decision, one that we had discussed at our board meeting a month before. If American women were to get the pill quickly, we would have to go it alone. We would have to produce three thousand doses immediately at our British plant, and clear them through FDA's required tests. I phoned the head of the FDA panel and asked if toxicology tests were enough, and whether our pharmacologist could agree on a test protocol with the FDA pharmacologist. Once the FDA approved our plan, we would resume British production. It would take seven or eight months. With a few more months for FDA clearance, we expected we could start trials with American women before the end of 1995.

It was a research project: we couldn't charge women for the pills. But despite the huge amount of money involved, we could prove that an American pill—made by us and financed by us—could be made available to American women in a remarkably short time. The aggressiveness of our approach might stall attempts by congressional extremists to ban RU 486. It would stir the enthusiasm of the abortion rights movement. It would be a backup resource for the Population Council, which might eventually want to use our British plant in case its contract with another plant ran into problems. There were risks at every turn, but we had been risktakers since the start of the movement, and this was probably the most critical of all.

12

Abortion and the Population Problem

The most puzzling and disturbing outcome of the RU 486 debate is that only a few countries have the legal right to distribute the pill to women using the French-made product. Except for France, the Hoechst-Roussel company has only licensed Britain and Sweden. China makes its own version of the drug, ignoring the international patent. Hoechst has totally divested itself of any American connections, giving the Population Council the patent.

Hoechst often looks like a company that wishes it hadn't stumbled into success. Obviously fearful of picket lines and other antiabortion attacks, it might be happier if the pill were kept in the laboratory and away from women. Much of the industrialized world is thus being penalized. But the punishment falls even harder on underdeveloped countries where access to vacuum abortion is often nonexistent. Here RU 486 could be an immeasurable boon. But so far Hoechst hasn't given the slightest indication that it wants to solve the needs of poor women. The excuse usually given is that the possibility of hemorrhaging from an RU 486 abortion endangers the lives of patients who are too distant from proper medical facilities. However, studies have shown that hemorrhages are extremely rare. Even this slight risk must be put into perspective. At least two hundred thousand women a year throughout the world, mainly in underdeveloped countries, die each year from botched abortions at the hands of quack practitioners and illegal clinics, according to the World Health Organization.[1]

No estimate has been made of the damage done to the health of surviving women or to their reproductive capacity. If the risks are weighed, women in underdeveloped countries would do far better to have RU 486 than continue to suffer the deaths and maimings of the present abortion underworld.

There is a reasonable alternative that would keep the risks to a minimum. Bangladesh offers one model. It has already trained thousands of medical technicians in an eighteen-month course to administer a government-supported program of "menstrual extraction" (MR). This technique involves the use of a bulb syringe attached to a flexible tube that is inserted into the womb. Administered within six to eight weeks of a missed menstrual period, MR "cleanses the uterine lining of any obstruction to menstruation," as government texts explain it, purposefully avoiding any comparison to a vacuum abortion.[2]

The striking conclusion from the Bangladesh model is that medical technicians have achieved a high level of safety and efficiency. One study, in fact, shows that female paramedics had only a 15 percent "complication rate" compared to 17 percent for the mainly male physicians.[3]

If paramedics can be trained in Bangladesh in a complex technique, they could certainly be trained elsewhere in the administration of RU 486. There will always be hurdles in the pill's multistep requirements. Poor transportation, for one, makes it harder for women to return for a check-up. Treatment, therefore, must be simplified by combining RU 486 and prostaglandin in one dose with a time release mechanism that would eliminate the need for an extra visit. Another move toward simplification would be to reduce the present French dose of 600 milligrams to 200 milligrams, which has already been approved in worldwide tests, and which would decrease the possibility of nausea, pain, and hemorrhage. "There is no question in my mind that 200 milligrams or less is enough of a dose," confirms Dr. Jose Barzelatto,[4] senior program advisor at the Ford Foundation and former director of the World Health Organization tests.

Hoechst must not be allowed to maintain RU 486 as an elitist drug. The failure to bring RU 486 to large numbers of women seems to stem more from bias than from its medical risks.

The public has not been educated to think of RU 486 as a valuable international resource in the way that citizens have been educated about voluntary sterilization. Yet sterilization has been transformed in a few decades from being an unknown technique to one with worldwide popularity. Today it is the number one form of birth control for at least 155 million people around the world, 16 million of whom live in the United States.[5]

Although sterilization involves surgery and some danger, particularly for women, it has never carried the stigma of abortions. The public looks at sterilization differently. Conception is blocked before sperm has met the egg. Nothing is damaged, not even a speck of fetal tissue is removed. Above all, it is a one-time procedure. By contrast, even though RU 486 only causes the shedding of the uterine lining, the general reaction is that a natural process has been stopped. A woman is escaping a birth she does not want, escaping the punishment that a male-dominated society thinks she must suffer for her pleasure. The proof of this clash in concepts can be found in the Catholic church itself. The papal encyclical *Casti Conubii* ruled in 1930 that individuals are "not free to destroy or mutilate their members" (a prohibition that the Vatican long overlooked when it allowed the removal of testicles for the Sistine Choir so that *castrati* voices would not gain their normal male pitch). Despite this Vatican ban on voluntary sterilization, many Catholic hospitals continued to perform it, including Sisters of Mercy hospitals in the United States. It was not until 1985 that the Vatican cracked down everywhere.

All of our prejudices concerning sterilization have been virtually erased in recent decades. It seems hard to believe that men and women once had to go through the ordeal of hospital approval committees similar to those whose members ruled on "therapeutic abortions." Sterilizations were rarely approved until people were in their mid-thirties. They usually required that a couple already had at least three or four children and a psychological investigation of a marriage's stability.

The women's movement, with its emphasis on the male's equal responsibility for birth control, soon shook up the old taboos. Lawsuits brought by the ACLU and the Association for Voluntary Surgical contraception added to the pressure on hospitals and doctors. The development of improved medical techniques hastened the change. At least one million Americans now choose sterilization each year.

Male vasectomy, involving the tying of the tubes in the testicles so that sperm cells cannot be ejected during intercourse, had always been a fairly simple, half-hour procedure under local anesthesia. Recently, it has been made even simpler by "no scalpel surgery" in which a doctor pierces the skin with an instrument and stretches the openings so that the tubes can be reached and blocked.[6] Female sterilization, which had long required at least an overnight hospital stay, was revolutionized in the 1960s by laparoscopy. Using a long, thin instrument inserted into the abdomen, the doctor could see the Fallopian tubes and then clip or cauterize them. The procedure could be done in an outpatient clinic and the woman could go home in a few hours.

Even the finality of sterilization has not diminished broad public acceptance. Every applicant is warned that because reversals are difficult, men and women must assume their days of childbearing and fathering are over. Few people, perhaps 2 percent, as a consequence of divorce, a partner's death, or the death of a child, seek reversals. Vasectomy reversals depend largely on how much of the vas or tube has been removed, but some skilled surgeons report a success rate of over 30 percent. Female reversals are more complicated; those sterilizations accomplished by plugs or rings are usually more successful than those resulting from chemical or electrical methods.[7]

Attitudes towards reversibility are now being altered further with the development of a new drug called Norplant. Consisting of six tiny capsules of progestin (sex hormones) implanted quickly and painlessly under a woman's skin, it inhibits ovulation and thus blocks pregnancy. Studies have shown Norplant implants to have a minuscule failure rate over five years.

The overwhelming advantage of Norplant is that a doctor can remove the capsules in half an hour, and a woman can become fertile again almost immediately Further, it contains no estrogen, thus eliminating some of the potential problems of hormonal impact on the system involved when using birth control pills.

Again, however, Norplant has produced the same problems of elitism that characterize the distribution of RU 486. Although developed in New York by the Population Council and tested for more than a dozen years on half a million women in sixteen countries, Norplant was not cleared by the FDA during the discriminatory Reagan-Bush era until 1990. Then its patent was released to Wyeth, a major drug company, which has kept its price so high that it is out of reach for the average woman.

In the United States, the capsules cost $350 (ten times what is charged in Finland), and insertion by a doctor usually runs $500 more. No attempt has been made to distribute Norplant widely in underdeveloped nations, where many women might consider it preferable to sterilization and where it certainly would be a major deterrent to abortion. At a time when soaring populations threaten the economic, social, and environmental stability of the world, the failure to bring Norplant and RU 486 to poor women is a critical blow to family planning.

Our attitudes toward the population crisis have also changed radically. Statistics and projections have the distant ring of Malthusian doom. We listen to United Nations' warnings that world population may exceed 6 billion by 1998, and 8.5 billion (at the low projection) to 9.1 billion (at the high projection) by the year 2025.[8] Yet such frightening figures have rarely made much of an impact on our daily lives. We have trouble linking them to the crime rate in Los Angeles or the deterioration of public housing in St. Louis.

Now, however, the high fertility rates in Somalia or Haiti have more meaning. We are beginning to realize the absurdity of sending U.N. and U.S. troops to pacify the warring factions in Somalia if its exploding population lacks enough food and other natural resources. Similarly, the restoration of democracy in Haiti depends on ending the country's poverty and overpopulation.

Peace in the Middle East remains threatened by the gap between population and natural resources. Cairo's population increases 7 percent annually; yet only 4 percent of Egypt is arable land. Saudi Arabia has lost one-fifth of its water reserve in the last decade, and Jordan consumes ground water one-and-a-half-times faster than it can be replenished.[9] Despite increasing concern with the interconnection of political stability and population, excess Turkish workers, once welcomed in Germany as cheap labor, are brutalized by neo-Nazis and skinheads.

One-fourth of the world lives in abject poverty, according to a World Bank study. Population control may be only part of the solution, but it is critical in India, Africa, and Southeast Asia, where 95 percent of our unchecked growth takes place. In India, where the population has leaped from 342 million in 1947 to more than 900 million today, and homeless hordes sleep in the streets of many cities, almost two-thirds of the urban poor have no drinking water. The World Watch Institute, a prominent observing group of environmentalists, estimates that 28 million tons of grain are needed annually to keep up with population growth, but only about 15 million tons are being produced.[10] If there is one, overriding conclusion from all these numbers, it is that the race between natural resources and population growth has become central to humanity.

Perhaps the key shift in attitudes stems from the women's movement. Family planning had always been considered a private choice, disconnected from the pressure of statistics. Now the impact of soaring populations has personalized the dangers to the health and survival of individual women and children. When women don't have access to birth control and abortion, they are forced to bear far more children than they can support, feed, and educate. Women's health becomes damaged through incessant childbirth. Their offspring are denied adequate nutrition, homes, and medical care.

"Women were breaking down under endless childbearing," pointed out Eleanor Smeal, president of the Feminist Majority, in 1994.

> They had little or no health care during pregnancy. Infant mortality rates in many countries had grown disastrous. We had to look at the total picture: How unchecked population growth demeaned the status of women and often ruined their lives.[11]

With one in twenty women in developing countries dying from pregnancy-related causes, compared with only one in ten thousand in industrialized countries, the most impressive outcome of the U.N. International Conference on Population and Development in Cairo in September 1994, was its emphasis on the empowerment of women.[12] The two previous conferences had virtually ignored this area. Now the reports covering reproductive rights and reproductive health care were lengthy and forceful.

The empowerment of women as a major factor in family planning, the importance and dignity society gives their lives, has become a reality in underdeveloped countries. Literacy particularly marks this change. One only has to compare the 88 percent literacy rate in Thailand and its 1.85 fertility rate (projected lifetime births per woman) against the shockingly low literacy rate of 14 percent in the Sudan and its high 5.0 fertility rate. India gives further proof. Its women are generally given little status, and rank low in literacy. Yet the state of Kerala on the southwestern coast of India is an exception. Advocating women's education, health, and legal rights, it has cut its birth rate to the level of China.[13]

The Cairo conference demonstrated that most of the world had come to grips with the increasing menace of overpopulation, and the U.S. Congress affirmed this commitment by approving President Clinton's $585 million donation to the U.N. population programs.

One of the failures of the conference, however, was that it talked a great deal about population control targets but decided on few practical programs to implement them. Even to reach the lower projected world population of 8.5 billion by the year 2025, all couples and individuals on earth would have to limit themselves to two children or less. In Africa, the total fertility rate would have to fall from 5.9 to 2.31; in India, it would have to fall from 3.06 to 2.04.[14] The conference's "Program for Action" abounded with phrases granting everyone the right to decide on the number of their children and their spacing. This is a long outdated luxury. The concentration should have been on incentives ranging from cash bonuses for voluntary sterilization to tax credits for those limiting themselves to two children. There was too little attention paid to the necessity of strong governmental initiatives such as those that have helped South Korea cut its total fertility rate from 5.0 to 1.6, and Kenya from 7.0 to 4.2.[15] Thailand celebrated its king's birthday uniquely on December 5, 1987, when a large Bangkok auditorium was divided into eight procedure rooms and twelve hundred men lined up, some for hours, to have their vasectomies.

Another conference failure was the attempt to placate the Vatican and its handful of Latin American and Muslim allies in dealing with abortion. The conference seemed tortured by the need to get unanimity on every issue, and to avoid an abortion clash. Still many delegates insisted that abortion, a reality almost everywhere, should not be cloaked under such disguises as "fertility regulation." Whether abortion was included or excluded as a method of family planning was unimportant. Women would seek abortion when necessary no matter what the language of the official report.

In the end, the compromisers won out. The official text confirmed:

> the right of women to be informed and to have access to safe, effective, affordable and acceptable methods of family planning of their choice, as well as other methods of their choice for the regulation of fertility, which are not against the law.[16]

Never had so much evasive wording been used to dodge a confrontation. A persistent question was why the Vatican continued to have such power for disruption. Its objective seemed to be to bring the conference to a halt by blocking any reference to abortion or even birth control. Was the Vatican trying to prove that it still had international power? Or that it could destroy the unity of a conference with endless wrangling? It might have been far more efficient for the conference to have approved its platform without the Vatican vote and perhaps a dozen other votes. This dissident faction was hardly essential to the population control campaign.

The fundamental issue was why the Vatican City merited a seat at the U.N. conference to begin with. Its minuscule 0.17-square-mile territory in the center of Rome could hardly be ranked as a country. Was it claiming authority as the State of the City of the Vatican (the terminology used in its Lateran Treaty with Italy in 1929)? Or did its authority stem from the spiritual entity of the Holy See? Either claim is dubious. The first meant that the U.N. and the United States were recognizing the religious ruler of a civil territory. The second had broad ramifications—if the Holy See deserved to be represented in a world organization, then the Anglican church could claim representation for its seat at Canterbury, England, and Islam could claim representation for its seat at Mecca.

This same, fundamental issue applied to the opening of a United States embassy at the Vatican in 1984. In its entire history, guided by the principle of separation of church and state, the American government had never appointed an ambassador to the Vatican. But under pressure from the Catholic-fundamentalist alliance, President Ronald Reagan breached this long-standing barrier. Despite a lawsuit brought by the National Council of Churches and many other groups, the U.S. District

Court, Eastern District of Pennsylvania, ruled that the president and Congress had total authority over foreign policy and embassy appointments.[17] Higher courts refused an appeal.

The Cairo Population Conference gave little heed to China, the one country that has made draconian efforts to cut its birth rate. With 22 percent of the earth's population and only 7 percent of its arable land, China by 1970 became frantically concerned that its numbers were far outstripping its agricultural and industrial resources. It launched a family planning initiative that halved its fertility rate but was no more than a palliative. In 1979, it moved to extreme measures with its "one child per family" campaign.

This was a drastic step, never attempted before by any country in history, and obviously only workable under a highly centralized, authoritarian regime. To limit couples to one child, the government imposed a web of punishments and inducements. Parents who obeyed the law were rewarded with benefits ranging from salary supplements to better housing. In rural areas, they got more land. Those disobeying the law were punished with everything from wage cuts to loss of social privileges.

China had the advantage of superior research laboratories and a sweeping network of birth control and abortion facilities. Its copy of the RU 486 pill was being tested on thousands of women. Still, abortion, particularly forced abortion, stirred controversy. American critics claimed that women, even in late pregnancy, were being physically dragged to clinics to stop a pregnancy. The government would later admit zealous local officials may have gone beyond accepted standards in the early years. But the government insisted such violations had ended, and foreign observers had little chance for accurate investigations of a huge bureaucracy.

Whatever its human rights record, China made astounding progress. In the cities, family size fell from 3.3 children per couple to 1.4. In the countryside, where farmers depended on a male child and authorities began to allow added pregnancies until a male child was born, family size only fell from 6.5 to 3.1 children.[18]

Admittedly, the one-child campaign disrupted Chinese society in many ways. The balance was being heavily tilted toward an aging majority, and the young would be heavily burdened to support benefits for the elderly. Female partners became difficult to find. Marriages were often postponed until people were in their thirties. Female babies were occasional victims of infanticide in rural areas.

Yet with all these complications, the Chinese experiment provides a model that may have to be followed elsewhere, at least in part. Only an authoritarian government, of course, could enforce it totally. Still, a system of democratic punishments and inducements will have to be adopted in such countries as India, where population pressures are severe. World population targets will never be met in the next half century until laissez-faire approaches are discarded and governments come to grips with a new concept of responsibility and crisis management.

The solution often comes from international cooperation. Uzbekistan and other central Asian republics, once part of the Soviet Union, recently recognized that their family planning programs were antiquated and dangerously limited. They invited the Association for Voluntary Surgical Contraception of New York, backed by U.S. aid money, to bring teams of experts on contraception and voluntary sterilization to their countries.

Now hospital and clinic staffs in this vast area are being trained in and supplied with the latest techniques.

Hypocrisy has to be replaced by reality. It seems fruitless for Americans to keep harping on China's human rights failures, particularly those stemming from the one-child family campaign, when the United States itself condones a form of human rights violations at home. Immigration policy here has not only become an expression of budget tightening, but of ridding states such as Florida and California of unwanted immigrants.

The soaring immigrant population of a few states may be a threat to the economy. But the way to control it is through intensified family planning, education, and industrial growth in the home countries. Stabilizing the earth's numbers cannot be achieved by pushing people back and forth across borders.

NOTES

1. Louise Silvestre et al., "Voluntary Interruption of Pregnancy," *New England Journal of Medicine,* March 8, 1990, vol. 322, no. 10, p. 645.

2. "Evaluation of Menstrual Regulation Services in Bangladesh," Bangladesh Association for the Prevention of Septic Abortion (BAPSA), Dhaka, 1987; other citations in Lawrence Lader, *RU 486,* Addison-Wesley, New York, 1991, fns. pp. 153–54.

3. R. Amin et al., "Menstrual Regulation in Bangladesh," *International Journal of Obstetrics & Gynecology,* vol. 27, 1988, pp. 265–71.

4. Author's interview with Dr. Jose Barzelatto.

5. Author's interview with Libby Antarsh, Association for Voluntary Surgical Contraception (AVSC), New York.

6. Jacques Rioux, Richard Soderstrom, "Sterilization Revisited," *Contemporary Ob-Gyn,* August 1987, pp. 80-104; Herbert Peterson et al.,

"Vasectomy: An Appraisal," *Obstetrics & Gynecology,* vol. 75, no. May 3, 1990, pp. 1–6.

7. Jaroslav F. Hulka et al., "Membership Survey on Laparoscopic Sterilization," *Journal of Reproductive Medicine,* vol. 35, no. 6, June 1990; Dana B. Schwartz et al., "Female Sterilization in the United States," *Family Planning Perspectives,* vol. 21, no. 5, Sept./Oct. 1989.

8. "The State of World Population: 1994," United Nations Population Fund, New York, 1993.

9. Pranay Gupte, *The Crowded Earth,* W.W. Norton, New York, 1984, p. 85; Dov Koch, "Middle East Water Crisis," *Midstream,* May 1993, pp. 16–19; Robert Engelman, Pamela LeRoy, *Sustaining Water,* Population Action International, Washington, D.C., 1993.

10. Shanti Conly, Sharon Camp, *India's Family Planning Challenge,* Population Crisis Committee, Washington, D.C. 1992.

11. Author's interview with Eleanor Smeal, Feminist Majority.

12. *International Dateline,* Population Communication International, New York, October 1994.

13. "International Human Suffering Index," Population Crisis Committee, Washington, D.C., 1992. Author's interview with Mike Klitsh, Alan Guttmacher Institute.

14. Donald Mann, "Cairo Conference on Population and Development," Negative Population Growth, Inc., Teaneck, New Jersey

15. "World Access to Birth Control," Population Crisis Committee, Washington, D.C., 1992.

16. *International Dateline,* op. cit.

17. *Americans United for Separation of Church and State v. Regan,* U.S. Dist., Ct., E. Dist., Pa., No. 84–4476, Complaint (1984); *American Baptist Churches* v. *Regan,* S. Ct. 86–113 (1986).

18. Shanti Conly, Sharon Camp, "China's Family Planning Program," Population Crisis Committee, Washington, D.C., 1992.

13

Abortion Rights and the Stand Against Compromise

Compromise has become so much a part of politics that we are apt to think of it as locked into law. This tradition must be opposed. Although most issues in the U.S. Congress and in state legislatures can be settled by horse-trading, political muscle, or other devices to bring about a consensus, there are certain areas of conflict that cannot be compromised. We might define these as moral and religious principles applying to the highest level of human conduct. We might propose that if a principle is right, it cannot be bargained away; that there are some truths that are so "self-evident" (in the words of the Declaration of Independence) that they stand above debate and alteration.

The obvious problem is what makes a truth self-evident and for whom? The statement in the Declaration of Independence that "all men are created equal" cannot be logically proved. Certainly, a fair number of colonists in 1776 rejected the Declaration of Independence and the Revolution itself, and stuck with the British empire. Similarly, the early abolitionists of the 1830s, who considered slavery the great moral and political stain on the nation, were branded a demented band at first, and had not even swayed a majority of the voters by the time the Civil War started.

Few groups in our history have based their actions on the "self-evident" concept. In addition to the abolitionists, the Quaker or pacifist who refuses military service is one example. The religious sect that refuses to swear allegiance to the government but only to God must be considered another. The only sanction for such stands is the validity of the cause. The only test of validity is that eventually its rightness will be written deep in the conscience of civilization.

Naturally, antiabortion groups, which believe that a fetus is a human person and that abortion is murder, may make the same claim to holding a "self-evident" truth. But their arguments have two major errors. First, the argument has no universal validity because most industrialized nations, and even some Catholic countries, support abortion rights. Second, whereas the prochoice stand is religiously neutral and does not require anyone to have an abortion against her conscience, antiabortion groups want their beliefs enforced by law. As long as they insist that the majority must yield to their convictions, and deny to others the right of free choice, there is no chance that the antiabortion position will ever achieve validity in the conscience of civilization.

If the anti-abortion platform some day achieves a majority of American opinion, it could insist its morality be written into law. A majority may not always be right, but it has the advantage of political power. Prochoice forces would then have to struggle to recapture majority opinion. In sum, truth may not always be a permanent rule and can often remain the battleground of politics. Self-evident truths may be the result of long and difficult conflict, the antislavery movement taking at least three decades before Lincoln's Emancipation Proclamation. We propose the thesis that refusal to compromise may be more than stubbornness. Drawing on the record of the abortion rights movement, we argue that refusal to compromise may often be the shortest route to success.

The critical moment came at the founding meeting of National Abortion Rights Action League (NARAL) in Chicago in February 1969, when a decision was made between "reform" and "repeal." The reform group of national delegates held out for a step-by-step approach, working for laws in each state (following the American Law Institute model) that would grant abortions to only a few thousand women locally, usually with the approval of a male-dominated medical committee. Legislatures in California, Colorado, and North Carolina had already put such laws on the books. It would be a painful process, swaying one legislature after another. But the reformers claimed the country was not ready for sweeping change, and that it would be years before most people could swallow the idea of a woman's total right to abortion.

By contrast, the repeal group would accept no compromise. It refused short-term approaches. It demanded immediate repeal of all laws that limited a woman's right of choice. Basing its arguments on the right of a woman to control her own body and procreation, it appealed to the law of personal liberty that was considered as sacrosanct for a woman in 1969 as for a slave in the 1830s. It also insisted that a woman's right to privacy was already protected by the Constitution, specifically by the Supreme Court's *Griswold* v. *Connecticut* decision on birth control in 1965 (although Federal Judge Robert Bork and similar interpreters could find no such privacy rights).

Going beyond these self-evident truths to practical politics, the repeal group argued that only a fight for total abortion rights could stir the imagination of the country. It was a concise, clear-cut stand. Now it was all or nothing. Women had been handed tidbits for too long, and only by exposing the sensitive nerve of women's demand to control their bodies could the new movement force the nation toward a great moral decision.

At Chicago in 1969, these two opposing philosophies clashed in a day of furious debate. At the end the repeal position won. It was a prescient decision for one of the most inflammatory social issues of the century. It gave the new movement idealism and moral strength, but it was also sound, practical politics. Although most observers thought it would take at least fifty years to repeal the old punitive abortion laws, it was done in seven years.

While the futility of rewriting history is obvious, there are numerous issues, slavery above all, which bear out the dangers of compromise and the thesis that self-evident truths should never be compromised. Certainly the prime example is the debate over slavery at the Constitutional Convention in 1787. Although many delegates were fervently opposed to slavery and wanted it outlawed, they ended up by imbedding it in three clauses of the Constitution, hypocritically neglecting to mention it by name. The nation, as a result, was torn apart for the next seventy-five years, and driven inevitably toward a bloody Civil War.[1]

Admittedly, the dominant impetus of the convention was to bind all thirteen states into a federal union, and this necessity overrode the sins of human bondage. Convinced that the new republic must protect property, the delegates were quick to yield to southern insistence that slaves were essential property.

All sorts of excuses were given for this disastrous compromise. Some delegates were convinced that slavery would fade away. Others favored the recolonization of slaves in Africa. Another logical alternative was that slaves could be purchased by the government and freed. "I would sooner subject myself to a tax for paying for all the negroes in the United States than saddle posterity with such a Constitution," insisted Gouverneur Morris, a Pennsylvania delegate. Yet this alternative was never seriously debated.

The most drastic solution—overridden by the conviction that the convention must do anything to hold the thirteen states together—was to oust the hardcore slave states immediately, and maintain the Declaration of Independence's principle that all men are created equal. This solution might not have damaged the new Union irreparably. It certainly would have avoided the coming decades of agony. "I think it wrong to admit in the Constitution the idea there can be property in men," proclaimed James Madison, who would eventually become the fourth president. "As much as I value the Union of all the States, I would not admit the Southern States into Union unless they agree to a discontinuance of this disgraceful [Slave] trade," asserted George Mason, prime author of the Virginia Bill of Rights.[2]

Despite the moral authority of these Virginians, the convention ignored the reality that only Georgia and South Carolina were inflexibly committed to slavery. Virginia and Maryland had already abolished the slave trade. North Carolina had partially abolished it.

If only two or three slave states had been excluded from the Union in 1787, the crisis that should have been apparent to the delegates might not have reached almost unsolvable dimensions by 1820. Through the slavery clauses of the Constitution and the Missouri Compromise of 1820, the Civil War was virtually predestined. The self-evident truth of the evil of slavery, which could have been solved rationally in 1787, would now have to be debated in blood. John Quincy Adams wrote presciently in 1820: "I have been among the most sanguine in believing that our Union would be of long duration. I now doubt it much."[3]

The most controversial aspect of any stand against compromise is the problem of deciding between competing truths. The night-riders of the Ku Klux Klan, who tortured and lynched blacks, claimed to be acting under their own version of self-evident truths. Similarly, the present right-to-life movement claims that abortion conflicts completely with its religious and ethical beliefs.

Lynching or the murder of abortion doctors or the burning of abortion clinics can never be tolerated. Yet all groups under the law deserve access to free speech and assembly in promoting their platforms.

In the end, what becomes a self-evident truth can only be decided by history and a consensus of conscience. Other countries may become a model. Slavery was abolished in Great Britain and elsewhere long before it was abolished in the United States. Abortion was legalized in Japan and Eastern Europe long before *Roe* v. *Wade,* and even Catholic countries such as Italy and Spain now have sweeping abortion rights laws. Thus the acceptance of self-evident truths is often influenced by world opinion.

But the final judgment must come from each unique situation. It seems unlikely that the Vatican or hard-core fundamentalists will ever cease to call abortion murder. What counts is when a consensus is formed among a majority of religious beliefs and ethical viewpoints, and that consensus becomes written into law by state legislatures and the Supreme Court. Self-evident truths are the product of struggle and even civil war. There may be setbacks along the way. One can imagine the possibility that the Republican, and basically antichoice, Congress elected in 1994 could try to curtail some of the rights guaranteed by *Roe* v. *Wade*. These rights, however, must never be compromised. For abortion rights, for separation of church and state, for any self-evident truth, the shortest route to justice is total struggle no matter how long it takes.

NOTES

1. For an analysis of the slavery debates at the Constitutional Convention, see Lawrence Lader, *The Bold Brahmins,* E.P. Dutton, New York, 1961, pp. 31–36.

2. For Gouverneur Morris, James Madison, George Mason, and other debates (only partially transcribed), see Max Farrand, ed., *The Records of the Federal Convention of 1787,* Yale University Press, New Haven, Connecticut, 1911. See also: Farrand, *The Framing of the Constitution of the United States,* Yale University Press, 1913; Jonathan Elliott, ed., *The Debates in the Several State Conventions on the Adoption of the Federal Constitution,* rev. 5 vols., Published under the Sanction of Congress, Washington, D.C., 1836–1845; and other citations in Lader, *Brahmins,* op. cit., pp. 302–303.

3. Lawrence Lader, "Mad Old Man from Massachusetts," *American Heritage,* April 1961, pp. 65–71.

14

Violence and Blood (1993 and 1994)

Violence and death haunted the abortion clinics in 1993 and 1994, diminishing the chance for any solution to the conflict that had ripped the country apart. In March 1993, Dr. David Gunn was shot to death by Michael Griffin in front of the Pensacola, Florida, clinic where Gunn performed abortions. The killer was convicted of first degree murder and given a life sentence.

On July 29, 1994, Dr. John B. Britton and James Barrett, a retired Air Force colonel who had served in three wars and was acting as Britton's escort, were shot to death in front of a second clinic in Pensacola, where the doctor performed abortions. Paul Hill, the killer, was given a life sentence in federal court for violating the victim's civil rights, and a death sentence in state court for murder.

The three assassinations marked a stage of deadly violence that had now become commonplace for anti-abortion extremists. They also clarified the desperate need for better security in clinics throughout the country. Although Dr. Britton was wearing a bulletproof vest, he was sitting in the car (not lying on the floor) as it pulled up to the clinic, and was shot in the head. There was no protective fence around the clinic entrance to shield arrivals, and Dr. Britton's schedule was not kept secret.

In the same week as Gunn's assassination, Dr. George W. Patterson, owner of one Pensacola clinic, who also practiced at other clinics, was shot to death in Mobile, Alabama, confronting a man breaking into his car. It may have been robbery. But since there was still cash on his body, the possibility of an abortion-related death could not be ruled out. Despite the arrest of the potential assassin, recently paroled from a life term in prison, and identified by witnesses near the car, there have been inexplicable delays. No trial had been held as of March 1995. Beyond the deaths themselves is the horrifying mind-set of those extremists who condoned the murders. The killing of abortion doctors and clinic staff members had long been excused as "justifiable homicide." "Of course David Gunn ought to have been drawn and quartered unto death," declared Michael Bray, already jailed for clinic obstruction, in *Capitol Area Christian News* in June 1993. "The noose of the prolife movement is tightening around Booker's neck," warned Charles Roy McMillan, referring to another abortion doctor, in the Dallas *Morning News* on May 29, 1994.

A petition advocating the use of lethal force against doctors and prochoice groups had been circulated by Paul Hill and signed by almost thirty others. Rev. David Trosch, one signer, who tried to place a newspaper ad advocating death for abortion doctors, announced: "If one hundred doctors need to die to save over one million babies, I see it as a fair trade."[1]

The extremists insistently equated the deaths of doctors and staff members with what they considered the death of babies in the womb. After the murder of Gunn, Don Treshman, national director of Rescue America, announced, "This shooting, while unfortunate, will result in babies' lives being saved."[2] Rochelle Shannon, an inveterate protester at clinics, wrote to Dr. Gunn's killer: "I know you did the right thing. . . . I wish I could trade places with you."[3] She lived out this deathly fantasy in August 1993 when she traveled to Wichita, Kansas, and fired two shots at clinic doctor George Tiller, wounding him. She was tried and jailed.

The objective of these killings was not just to eliminate a single doctor from performing additional abortions; it was meant to strike fear into all clinic doctors and staff members, who might well expect that the next shot could be fired at them. It was becoming harder to find doctors with the commitment to work at a clinic. Vacuum abortion training had been dropped from so many curricula at medical schools that groups like New York City Planned Parenthood were setting up courses of their own.

"It is not the demonstrations that I fear," stated Dr. Warren Hern, head of a Colorado clinic, who suffered one attempt on his life, had five bullets fired through his waiting room window, and now wears a bulletproof vest. "It is the lone fanatic who steps out of the shadows to deliver the ultimate message of hatred for what I do to help women."[4]

Most of the mainstream anti-abortion groups, particularly the Catholic church, expressed their dismay at the killings. Some groups temporarily called off demonstrations outside of clinics. But was this enough? In an atmosphere of hatred that had been built up around clinics for years, in a frenzy of epithets of "murderer" and "killer" hurled at patients as they entered clinics and were blocked violently by demonstrators, wasn't the scene set for the fury of an assassin?

The trappings for terror had been created increasingly throughout 1994. Two clinics in Redding and Chico, California, were doused with gasoline and set ablaze. The office of Dr. James Armstrong in Kalispell, Montana, was firebombed. He was the third abortion provider in Montana whose facility had been burned since 1992. The attacks ranged from the burning of a Planned Parenthood clinic in Brainerd, Minnesota, to the firebombing of a Falls Church, Virginia, clinic.[5] In a survey by the Feminist Majority Foundation, answered by 314 clinics in late 1994, almost 25 percent reported death threats to their staff, and almost 52 percent experienced one or more types of violence.

The most fervent of the protesters are often spotted moving from clinics in one city to clinics in another. Susan Hill, who runs eight clinics in the National Women's Health Organization, reported that the same protesters appeared recently in Milwaukee, Wisconsin; Fort Wayne, Indiana; and Fargo, North Dakota. They are obviously well-funded although claiming to have no money. "There is no difference between this group of traveling terrorists and groups of terrorists in the Middle East," Hill declared.[6]

It didn't seem possible that the year could bring further horror. Yet it came again from a gunman who police found had attended at least one meeting of the Massachusetts Citizens for Life, a loner whose fanaticism had obviously been stirred by mounting bloodshed. It took place not in an anti-abortion stronghold like Pensacola, but in Boston, Massachusetts, one of the leading prochoice cities in the country.

On December 29, 1994, a black-clad gunman strode into the Planned Parenthood clinic on Beacon Street in suburban Brookline and shot the twenty-five-year-old female receptionist to death. Then he raced, probably by car, to Preterm Health Services on the same street a mile away, and shot another staff woman nine times. She died in the hospital. Five other people at both clinics were wounded.

The suspect, twenty-two-year-old John C. Salvi III, quickly identified from a gunshop receipt left behind, then drove to Norfolk, Virginia, and allegedly opened fire on the Hillcrest Clinic, which has long been the target of violent demonstrations. Quickly apprehended by local police, he was extradited to Boston a few days later.

Salvi seemed to fit the profile of the true fanatic. He was strongly motivated by religion, carrying on the back of his pickup truck an oversized picture of Jesus Christ as an aborted fetus, writing in a rambling note from jail that if he was not convicted, he wanted to train as a Catholic priest.[7] Yet so many of his actions and background seemed to cross the line into madness that he could possibly seek an insanity defense. Here was the terrible forewarning of future killings.

Many potential extremists, particularly those in groups condoning murder, can be identified by the FBI and other authorities and closely watched. But it is the lone fanatic, lurking in the dark, who presents the hidden danger to law enforcement. Clinic security would become an increasingly agonizing problem.

It is not easy to analyze why the extremist mentality has exploded into murder within such a short time period. Perhaps the twelve years of the Reagan-Bush presidencies, with the expectation of anti-abortion successes, kept zealots from taking drastic steps. Perhaps Bill Clinton's election on a prochoice platform, and the passage of the Freedom of Access to Clinic Entrances bill providing clinic protection, stirred extremist frustrations to the breaking point. Firebombing may have seemed no longer effective. The ultimate religious zealots, convinced they represented the only righteous course against the evil of abortion, moved to a new level of desperation, with the power of the gun becoming the route to personal salvation. Each assassin was certain that a bullet would prove to be a personal apocalypse, an essential step in saving his soul as well as the country, even if it meant a life in prison or possible execution.

Interestingly, except for presidential assassinations, there are few such patterns in U.S. history. People have rarely killed over a specific social issue. The Los Angeles riot deaths seemed to have stemmed from the pent-up anger of the poor against economic deprivation. Murders and lynchings in the South for many decades after the Civil War aimed at reenslaving black people, and had the virtual sanction of state and local antiblack laws. The same protective sanction of regional laws cloaked the violence and murders of civil rights workers in the 1960s.

John Brown's bloody campaign against slavery before the Civil War constitutes the closest parallel to the present abortion killings. His Harper's Ferry raid, attempting to start a slave rebellion in Virginia, resulted in a score of deaths. The difference, of course, is that Brown used violence against a slave system that had millions of victims and that most of the civilized world had already banned. Brown's vehemence aimed at the rescue of human beings, not fetuses. Union troops went into battle singing "John Brown's Body," and history, more often than not, excuses the bloodshed he caused. Almost no one, by contrast, can find a philosophical basis for the clinic killings. If we started approving murder over a social issue, there might soon be people killing doctors for participating in the legalized suicides recently approved by an Oregon law.

It is hard to find a way to deal with the psychology of abortion extremists. My own approach has been to push birth control, always arguing in public debates that if better contraception was made available to everyone, we could quickly cut the number of abortions in half. This reasoning rarely works, for most extremists are as vehemently opposed to birth control as they are to abortion. We are dealing with an inexhaustible hatred against the right of a woman to control her body and procreation, and I suspect that such hatred can only be met by strong laws and strong institutional condemnation.

Two institutions that could blunt extremist anger are the Catholic church and the Republican party. While Catholic bishops have deplored the abortion killings, they have done little to temper the aura of violence that incites such acts. In fact, Planned Parenthood of New York City cited Cardinal John O'Connor for issuing a "backhanded apology for the attackers by stating 'you cannot prevent killing by killing,' thereby labeling abortion providers as killers."[8]

Even though the Catholic church has a perfect right to oppose abortion from the pulpit and from street corners, it has a responsibility not just to prevent murder, but to prevent right-to-life groups from physically blocking patients from entering a clinic, from pursuing patients and staff members to their homes, from destroying their property, and hounding them with vengeful phone calls. There will never be any sanity to the abortion debate if the Catholic bishops cannot shift the plane from one of violence to one of constitutional standards of free speech.

The Republican party, too, has a similar responsibility. Such leaders as Gov. Pete Wilson in California and Gov. William Weld in Massachusetts have kept the abortion debate on a flexible and tolerant course. After the credit given the women's movement for a sizeable role in Bill Clinton's election in 1992, the Republican party seemed to be moving toward the mainstream. The 1994 elections stopped all that. The hard-core Republican vote was attributed to the Christian right, which is almost solidly anti-abortion. In the South and increasingly elsewhere, the Christian right dominates party machinery. There are exceptions, of course. U.S. Rep. Susan Molinari of Staten Island, New York, remains highly conservative but prochoice. Still, the 104th Congress could well become the most anti-choice Congress in history.

The Christian Coalition claims to have distributed thirty-three million voter guides before the 1992 elections. While the guide stopped short of actually endorsing candidates, they rated candidates by their stands on issues relevant to the Christian right, most particularly abortion. Given the Christian Coalition's tax-exempt status, this guide could be a potential violation of the Internal Revenue Service's rules. Many churches, passing out the guide to parishioners at services, could be identified as lawbreakers.

Significantly, this growing partnership between the Christian right and the Republican party was successful in electing hard-line anti-abortionists in the Florida area where the assassinations of clinic doctors took place: Joe Scarborough in Pensacola and David Weldon in nearby Cape Canaveral, who defeated a pro-choice Democrat. Both districts previously had Democrat incumbents.

Most of the newly elected Republican senators, notably in Ohio, Oklahoma, and Pennsylvania, ran on vehement, Christian right platforms. Strong conservatives often replaced moderate Republicans. In the end, at least five senators and forty House members who supported freedom of choice were replaced by extreme anti-abortionists.

The three agencies that could be crucial in stopping the abortion clinic violence are the U.S. attorney general, the FBI, and the local police and courts. Yet by the middle of 1995, their effectiveness had been only modest. The National Women's Health Organization (NWHO) with its eight clinics has obtained over a thousand arrests of violent demonstrators and has spent over $500,000 in legal fees. But of the $100,000 in damages and fees awarded by the courts, the organization has collected nothing. Of 455 arrests in Fort Wayne, Indiana, charges have been dropped in all cases. In Milwaukee, there were only twenty prosecutions out of 2,100 arrests.

Although federal marshals have been placed at many clinics since the Boston assassinations, there is a lack of commitment in some areas. "We have had arsons at our eight facilities and only one arrest by federal authorities," Susan Hill of NWHO told the House subcommittee on crime.

> They commonly ask us to close our clinics for the day so they won't have to deal with the problem. They have told us they are tired of spending so much money arresting these people, only to see charges dropped.

"The local police tell us the feds should do this, the feds tell us the local authorities have jurisdiction," Hill continued. After a federal judge put a buffer zone around her clinic in Fort Wayne a few years ago, and ordered the police to read the injunction every morning, "the police have refused to read the injunction. The U.S. attorney refused to bring contempt charges saying he had no jurisdiction to enforce this injunction." Of what value has the Freedom of Access to Clinic Entrances act been in protecting Ms. Hill's clinics? Two U.S. Attorneys "told us that FACE was virtually useless," Hill concluded.

I was sitting in the Pensacola Ladies Center with Linda Taggart, the clinic director, in January 1995 when a phone call came in from the Florida Department of Law Enforcement. The agent warned her that boxes had just been mailed to Florida clinics. They contained ceramic guns and threatening notes that future boxes would contain bombs. "No packages or bulky mail should be opened," the agent instructed. The phone call was just one example of the pall of fear surrounding Pensacola's clinics. It had only been six months since Dr. Britton's assassination at the Ladies Center. A bomb had exploded there on June 25, 1984, forcing the clinic to close for six months to repair the damage. On Christmas day that year, further bombs ripped the clinic, as well as the offices of two doctors who were known to have performed abortions. A note at the site announced that the bombs were a "gift to Jesus on his birthday." On May 17, 1988, John Brockhoeft was arrested by police, carrying bombs en route to the same clinic. He was convicted and sentenced to jail.

Pensacola is truly a city under siege. It is a remarkable testament to the staying power of the clinics that they have been able to replace their murdered doctors. After Dr. Gunn was murdered at Pensacola Women's Medical Services, one doctor telephoned quickly to volunteer. Another took special training so that he could qualify to do abortions under Florida's medical standards.

The staff members of these clinics, unfortunately, have begun to bend under the pressure. Two of Taggart's five nurses have left. Her patient counselor for seventeen years is looking for another job. Taggart, a petite woman, fifty-six years old, with dazzling blue eyes, had employed her daughter at the clinic. But after the daughter married and had a child, she could only avoid harassing phone calls by keeping her married name secret and out of the phone book.

There is no doubt that fanatics have concentrated on Pensacola, determined to drive the clinics out of the city. John Burt, an ex-Klansman and one of the most violent demonstrators, constantly pickets the home of Sandy Sheldon, administrator of Women's Medical Services. He was arrested and sentenced to sixty days in jail for trespassing on clinic property. Burt followed Dr. Gunn's car and took the photograph of him that was featured on the provocative "Unwanted Gunn" poster, displayed everywhere just months before Gunn's assassination. On a video camera, the clinics also have a picture of Burt seemingly identifying Dr. Britton to Paul Hill, who shot the doctor shortly thereafter.

Burt was part of the group that invaded the Ladies Center a few years ago. "They pushed me down," Taggart recalls. "I tried to block Burt's way, but he pushed me aside and shoved his arm across my neck." Joan Andrews, another frequent demonstrator, vandalized the clinic in March 1985, and caused

$1,800 worth of damage.[9] She was convicted and sentenced to five years.

Zealots constantly follow the clinic's staff when they drive home from work. When Pat Welch, a pretty, dark-haired worker at Ladies Center, and her sister, Paula, were picking up their children at a dancing school in January 1995, a man they recognized from previous demonstrations parked near them, and shouted, "Don't mess with me. I can give you trouble."

The speciality of these extremists is to identify doctors who perform abortions. Andrew Burnett in his publication *Life Advocate* constantly publishes a list of doctors, including their addresses and phone numbers, and describes how Paul Hill tracked down Dr. Britton. But their pressure tactics extend to clinic insurance and real estate. When the Women's Clinic in Fort Lauderdale, Florida, signed a lease with a seemingly sympathetic landlord and spent twenty thousand dollars on renovations, Joyce Tarnow, the clinic owner, found there had been such harassment of the landlord that she was locked out on moving day. She was forced to find another location with a more committed landlord.

Real estate pressure by anti-abortionists has become a pattern. In Garden City, New York, in March 1995, a landlord tried to evict Long Island Gynecological Services from his building although the lease still had eight years to run. He claimed that he had no objection to abortion but was simply trying to protect other tenants in his building from picket lines and potential violence. The case remained unsettled in mid-1995.

In Pensacola, Vicky and Mike Conroy, Roman Catholics and parents of ten children whom they insist on educating at home, claim to be the leading "hunters" of doctors. They are always at the airfield, trying to identify doctors commuting from other cities. The police now meet doctors on the plane, cover their faces, and escort them to a waiting police car. But after a doctor's plane recently arrived early, and the Conroys were able to snap the physician's picture in the waiting lounge, the police have established a secret rendezvous room in case they fail to meet the plane.

The Conroys identified Dr. Britton's license plate, and they boast of finding Dr. Steven Chase Brigham working at a Pensacola clinic after his New York medical license was revoked, and his practice halted in New Jersey until an administrative law judge rules on his competence. The clinic denies that he worked there. The Conroys "may not pull the trigger but they are fanning the flames," says Sandy Sheldon of Pensacola Women's Medical Services. The extremist ranks are constantly replenished by recruits from other parts of the country: for example, Robert Cook of Wisconsin. Because the Ladies Center parking lot is small, a patient's driver is usually escorted to the drugstore parking lot nearby. Cook recently followed an escort there, shouting, "Does the drugstore have bulletproof glass?"[10]

Another turbulent visitor is Rev. David Trosch, a sixty-eight-year-old Catholic priest who ministers to a small church outside Mobile, Alabama. A portly man with wire-rimmed glasses and a receding, gray hairline, Trosch announced after the three Pensacola murders, "I would say that Paul Hill and Michael Griffin had special callings from God to do exactly what they did." Now Trosch has gone a step further, urging the execution of patients. "If half a dozen women were executed for having abortions, you'd just about stop abortions in this country,"[11] Trosch told a Pensacola *New Journal* reporter.

That paper's editorial urged that Trosch receive the "full weight of church punishment up to and including excommunication." Because Trosch still calls himself director of Defensive Action, a group advocating the killing of abortion doctors, the same reporter asked Archbishop Oscar Lipscomb of Alabama whether he intended to excommunicate Trosch. Lipscomb evaded a direct answer.

Such evasions are symptomatic of the way the Catholic hierarchy (and almost all religious denominations in Pensacola) mouth platitudes against these assassinations, but do nothing to oppose the threats. The number of fundamentalist churches in Pensacola is one of the largest in the country for a city with a population of 65,000. Pete Hamill, who took his naval flight training there, wrote in an *Esquire* article that "religion seems to stain the very air." Although three fine hospitals and the military bases lend an edge of sophistication to the city, the only denomination to come out determinedly for abortion rights (with a bit of help from a Methodist minister and Jewish rabbi) is the Unitarian-Universalist church. Such groups as the Episcopalians and the Presbyterians, which are critical to the Religious Coalition for Abortion Rights on a national level, have remained disturbingly silent.

"I don't think people care about clinic violence," observes Ginny Graybiel of the *News Journal.* "It's as though a shroud covers everything, and the only bad things are done by bad people from out of town," concludes Dallas Blanchard, retired Methodist minister, now chair of the Sociology and Anthropology Departments at the University of West Florida.[12]

One puzzling issue concerns the financial backing for these purveyors of violence. Paul Hill, a defrocked minister who seemed to have no regular source of income, paid $72,000 in cash for his house. Three days before he shot down Dr. Britton, his wife withdrew $10,000 from their bank account.[13] Many of the fundamentalist churches are well-funded by their parishioners, and their zeal against abortion was demonstrated by a First Assembly of God minister's clash with police, which almost got him indicted. It seems hard to believe that incessant lawbreakers like Rochelle Shannon, now in jail for wounding Dr. Tiller, could attack nine clinics in widely separated cities with acid and other specialized technology unless they were financed and guided by a central source. Still, the FBI, which has been investigating the conspiracy theory, has produced no hard evidence.

The most distinguishing characteristic of these fanatics is that they are often prone to violence, not only against abortion rights, but in their own personal lives. Michael Griffin, killer of Dr. Gunn, was described as violent in court papers filed by his wife, Patricia, in 1991. Stephen Butler, an Operation Rescue leader, often arrested at demonstrations, was jailed in Livermore, California, recently for beating his wife, kicking her in the head, and throwing a metal chair at her that injured their child.[14]

Clinics in Pensacola and Boston, sites of the recent assassinations, and clinics everywhere, have come to realize that they can no longer afford a minuscule slip in security. Not just doctors but most staff members and volunteer escorts generally wear bulletproof vests. Video cameras cover a wide sweep of ground around each clinic. When I visited Sandy Sheldon at Women's Medical Services, a federal marshal at the front door checked my identity and brief case. The same procedure was followed inside the door by a clinic staff member. There is a second marshal at the back door. The clinic is located in a fashionable complex of two-story, gray buildings containing offices and stores. Because most of the area is private, demonstrators must stay on the public road about sixty feet away, and patients are instructed to drive to the back door, which is private and totally secure.

By contrast, the Ladies Center, a two-story, dark-rust wood building, is located on a major highway with steady traffic. These demonstrators can occupy public property almost at the front door. Although a federal marshal always sits in a car in the adjoining parking lot, marshals vary in their commitment; while I was there, one man entered the clinic without being checked. For a long time, Paul Hill owned a strip of land next to the parking lot, where he erected a high platform and he sat with a bullhorn screaming threats at entering patients. The police finally banned the platform.

Sandy Sheldon, a constantly smiling southerner who insists you can't tell a Florida sheriff what to do but must woo him with graciousness, has spent a lot of money on her clinic's electronic warning system, alarms, video surveillance, and bulletproof glass. She is typical of the clinics under siege. Susan Hill in an interview in the *Wall Street Journal* pointed out that her Fargo, North Dakota, clinic took in $500,000 last year but spent $536,000, much of it on increased rent and insurance, legal costs, and private security guards. Video surveillance generally costs from $5,000 to $10,0000, a metal detector $4,500, and security guards $25 an hour. Dr. Warren Hern, director of a clinic in Boulder, Colorado, reports that he spent $1 million on security in recent years.

"The old police chief was just never around," observes Ginny Graybiel of the Pensacola *News Journal.* But the new police chief, Norman Chapman, has strengthened the commitment of his force. The City Council has finally passed an ordinance establishing a protective zone eight feet around each clinic in which only the police can stand.

Despite the police and marshals at some locations, clinics increasingly have had to transform themselves into armed bastions. After his former clinic in downtown Reno—the only one in northern Nevada—was firebombed four times, Dr. Damon Stutes has put $1 million into his new West End Women's Medical Group. It has solid steel doors; magnetic locks; infrared motion detectors; bulletproof windows, and panic buttons for summoning the police. The patient parking lot is set well back from the street. Stutes checks his video screens, covering all surrounding streets before he puts on his bulletproof vest, checks his Beretta pistol, and takes his high-speed truck from the garage. Pistols may hardly be standard gear yet, but K. B. Kohls of the Beacon Women's Center in Montgomery, Alabama, may be the first woman administrator to carry a gun.

Federal marshals are an integral part of security, but there are not enough of them to guard every clinic in the country. In fact, after the shock of the Pensacola killings had worn off, there were only ten clinics being guarded in November 1994. The Boston killings stirred the government to increase federal protection, particularly after Eleanor Smeal of the Feminist Majority revealed that twenty-one clinics had just received death threats. It has become a grim tug-of-war with clinics warning of potential assassins and the government, under Republican budget-cutting pressure, trying to curb abortion rights expenditures.

Despite the FACE act's provisions for protecting clinic access, and the nonbinding Senate resolution of January 1995 calling for FACE's strict enforcement, the constant problem is to get immediate action under the law.

Linda Taggart of the Pensacola Ladies Center, for example, tried and failed to get Paul Hill arrested under the provisions of FACE about four weeks before he killed Dr. Britton.[15] Not only is responsibility often bandied back and forth between federal officials and local police, but the rulings of federal judges can be ignored. Now Susan Hill, who already described this morass to a congressional committee, is testing the federal system again. In January 1995 she got the U.S. attorney to go to court against two demonstrators who barred access to her Fargo, North Dakota, clinic with old cars and scrap metal. If the federal judge approves the requested two-hundred-foot safety zone around the clinic and marshals enforce the ruling, it may set a precedent for safety zones nationwide.[16]

The ultimate power of enforcement, in the end, must come from U.S. Attorney General Janet Reno. Unless she lays down strict directives that the FACE act must be obeyed scrupulously, and the orders of federal judges carried out, clinics will remain the victims of the evasions and temporizings that have been going on for a year.

Although a few clinic directors like Charlotte Taft in Texas have refused to inflict a battlefield mentality on their clients, the reality is that every clinic, as well as the prochoice movement supporting it, has been plunged into a state of war. Clinics increasingly depend on the escort troops supplied by the movement. In Pensacola, 350 escorts have been trained by Debbie Myers, a clinic aide, and Bill Caplinger, a volunteer who works as the manager of laboratories at the University of West Florida.

Most escorts wear bulletproof vests. They are skilled at shielding patients and drivers from harassment, getting clients inside the door quickly, and parking their cars. One escort is an eighty-year-old man; another, a sixteen-year-old boy who reports regularly with his parents. The principal sources of volunteers are the local colleges, the Unitarian church, and the NOW chapter, which has about a hundred members.

Chicky Desmarais, president of the Pensacola NOW chapters, a registered nurse who spent six years in the navy as an electronics communications expert, was driving to the Ladies Center for escort duty the morning Dr. Britton was assassinated. If she hadn't been held up a few minutes by highway construction, she would have been in the parking lot when the shots were fired.

"I saw June Barrett all bloody being put in an ambulance, she said. "I thought it was a bombing. I stood there, paralyzed, and finally sunk down on my knees and started to cry."[17]

On January 22, 1995, the day I arrived in Pensacola, the twenty-second anniversary of the *Roe* v. *Wade* decision, an extremist group known as the American Coalition of Life Activists announced their new "hit list." Among the twelve doctors providing abortions who were accused of "crimes against humanity" was Dr. Warren Hern of Colorado, who had helped organize the National Abortion Rights Action League with me in 1969.

NOTES

1. Pensacola *News Journal,* August 30, 1994, p. 1A; *New York Times,* August 18, 1993.

2. *New York Times,* August 20, 1993, p. A12.

3. *New York Times,* October 25, 1994, p. A19; *New York Times,* August 22, 1993, sec. 1, p. 29

4. *New York Times,* op-ed, August 12, 1993, p. A25.

5. *Reproductive Freedom News,* October 21, 1994, p. 4; September 9, 1994, p. 8

6. Author's interview by phone with Susan Hill.

7. *New York Times,* January 1, 1995, p. A27.

8. Planned Parenthood of New York City, ad in *New York Times,* January 5, 1995, p. A17.

9. Author's interview with Linda Taggart.

10. Author's interview with Chicky Desmarais (Pensacola NOW). For Conroys: Pensacola *News Journal,* January 22, 1995, p. 8A.

11. Pensacola *News Journal,* August 30, 1994, p. 1A, 4A; August 18, 1994, p. 4A and editorial.

12. Author's interview with Ginny Graybiel and Dallas Blanchard.

13. Author's interview with Desmarais.

14. Pensacola *News Journal,* March 11, 1993; *Freedom Writer,* February 1995, p. 8.

15. Pensacola *News Journal,* July 31, 1994, p. 1.

16. U.S. Dist., Ct., S.E. Div., No. Dak, Civil Action A-3, 95–4, L8 January 1995.

17. Author's interview with Desmarais.

This chapter is based mainly on interviews with Dallas Blanchard, Bill Caplinger, Chicky Desmarais, Ginny Graybiel (who kindly provided access to the Pensacola *News Journal* clipping files), Susan Hill (by phone,) Debby Myers, Sandy Sheldon, Linda Taggart, Caroline Tesche, and Pat Welch.

15

Methotrexate:
Another Abortion Drug,
Another Choice for Women

Methotrexate seemed to appear from nowhere and achieved national prominence in 1994. Actually, it has been used for psoriasis for more than forty years and has been prescribed to combat cancer and severe arthritis. Most importantly, it has become an increasingly effective treatment for ectopic pregnancies, the dangerous mishap when a fetus starts to grow in a Fallopian tube instead of the uterus. Only in the last few years have researchers proved Methotrexate's value as an abortifacient, yet early studies date back to the 1950s, and, oddly enough, I described them in my book *Abortion* in 1966.[1]

Methotrexate's meteoric ascendency can be attributed to the long and tortured process of bringing RU 486 to American women nation-wide. Its great advantage is that it has long been approved by the FDA for other uses and thus is now available to clinicians.

Another advantage is its low cost. One dose runs only about $5, and the prostaglandin, taken with it to intensify the action, costs about $2. Although no one knows what the Roussel company charges per pill, the charge per woman for RU 486 treatment in France is about $300 and in Britain it's about $500. The charge in the United States may be similar, depending on what company gets the license to manufacture and distribute the drug.

Although methotrexate and RU 486 have had equally impressive success rates as abortifacients, their methods of bringing on an abortion are completely different. By acting on the body's progesterone hormone receptors, RU 486 causes bleeding by shedding the inside lining of the uterus. Methotrexate blocks the use of folic acid, a vitamin needed by the rapidly growing fetal cells, and thus causes fetal death.

RU 486 is administered orally by pill, methotrexate is given by injection. Both require a followup dose of misoprostol, a prostaglandin, a few days later. Methotrexate researchers have found it more effective when the prostaglandin is given intravaginally.

Although methotrexate, as an agent against cancer, is a highly potent drug, the dosage for abortion is significantly lower. All current tests are aimed at proving its safety as well as its efficiency. Yet it has gone through less than a thousand trials, which puts it at a disadvantage to RU 486, which has already been used on at least two hundred thousand patients in France, Britain, Sweden, China, and in World Health Organization studies.

On the other hand, methotrexate already has a distinguished record of safety in the treatment of thousands of cases of early, unruptured ectopic pregnancies. It is now accepted as a decided advance over the old surgical method of laparoscopy in which the doctor inserts a tiny instrument into the woman's body and removes the pregnancy from the Fallopian tube. Laparoscopy usually requires a three-day hospital stay. Methotrexate does not require hospitalization and sharply reduces the recovery period.

The impact on medical progress has been remarkable. From 1970 to 1989, the number of ectopic pregnancies have more than tripled, reaching 88,400 in 1989. Moreover, ectopic pregnancies account for 13 percent of all pregnancy-related deaths, making it one of the leading causes of maternal mortality. Not only has methotrexate treated ectopic pregnancies successfully in 95 percent of early unruptured cases, but it has no effect on future pregnancies. Almost 80 percent of women wanting a child after taking methotrexate became pregnant in 1.1 to 3.2 months. Low cost is a particular bonus. While surgical treatment of ectopic pregnancies average about $7,972, methotrexate runs only about $1,495 if hospitalization is required, and much less if it is not. Extrapolating these figures to the nationwide number of procedures, researchers estimate that the annual savings by using methotrexate for ectopic pregnancies would be in excess of $280 million.[2]

It is little wonder that several years ago researchers became excited about the use of methotrexate as an abortifacient. The Roussel company of France had consistently refused to bring RU 486 to American women, and methotrexate seemed to be a propitious alternative that was immediately available. Simple to administer, the drug was easily given in a doctor's office, which would guarantee the privacy of a woman against the increasing anti-abortion attacks on hospitals and clinics.

The principal researchers are Dr. Philip Darney at the University of California, San Francisco, and his former partner, Dr. Mitchell Creinin, now at the University of Pittsburgh; Dr.

David Grimes at the University of Southern California; and Dr. Eric Schaff at the University of Rochester. All of them carried on their work under official review boards at their institutions. In New York, however, Dr. Richard Hausknecht failed to come to an agreement with the prestigious hospital where he taught. A veteran of the New York abortion rights movement, he was so convinced of the value of methotrexate that he decided to treat patients on his own in his office.

In a 1993 study by Creinin and Darney, all patients who received a dose of methotrexate determined by their height and weight, followed by prostaglandin, "had rapid expulsion of the uterine products and 83 percent had a complete abortion." The side effects were limited to mild abdominal cramping, and vaginal bleeding, although prolonged, was reduced to "spotting" after the tenth day.[3]

In a 1994 study by Creinin and Eric Vittinghoff, the success rate rose to 90 percent, with more than 60 percent of the patients aborting on the same day that prostaglandin was administered. Again, "undesired side effects" were "infrequent."[4]

Schaff's 1994 study was noteworthy for achieving over a 98 percent success rate. The higher rate might be explained because he concentrated on the first seven weeks of pregnancy while Creinin went up to eight weeks. Schaff uses the standard pregnancy tests instead of a vaginal, ultrasound machine for pregnancy detection. It is not only expensive, costing about $300, but the required intravaginal probe is unappealing to many patients, and the inclusion of the radiology staff brought a loss of privacy and added to the time of the procedure. This may not be a problem for gynecologists with office ultrasound.

Schaff is responsible for another innovation. He had the prostaglandin made into a vaginal suppository, which meant that patients could administer the second drug themselves at home on the third day, thus eliminating an office visit.

Thirty-six of fifty-four subjects had an immediate response to prostaglandin. Bleeding started an average of 7.4 hours after the drug was administered. Like the previous studies, vomiting and diarrhea were minimal. Perhaps the most striking conclusions of the study were that all but two subjects reported that the procedure was acceptable, and all but one would choose the procedure over a surgical abortion in the future.[5]

In his protocol, or plan, for his studies, Schaff describes the procedure to each patient on day one, has her sign a consent form, and gives her a urine pregnancy test and other medical checkups, including a blood pregnancy level test to make sure that the fetus is eight weeks old or less. Schaff then injects the patient with methotrexate, and supplies her with a suppository of prostaglandin to take home, instructing her to insert it deep into the vagina, rest on her back for thirty minutes, and expect cramping and bleeding in the next twelve hours.

On day seven, the patient returns to Schaff's clinic for another blood pregnancy level test. If sufficient bleeding has occurred, and there is a significant drop in blood pregnancy levels, the abortion is completed. The patient will be considered an "immediate responder." Otherwise, she may be given a second suppository to complete the abortion.

These late-responding women return to Schaff on day fourteen. If blood pregnancy levels show the abortion as uncompleted, they will be given an ultrasound exam. In the first fifty cases of Schaff's 1994 study of a hundred patients, all had successful abortions except for one, who was inadvertently included despite being beyond fifty-six days of gestation. She had to have a surgical abortion.

An impressive part of Schaff's study is that he estimates the cost per woman, including office visits and testing, at $125. This compares with about $500 for a surgical abortion (higher in some parts of the country), and probably a similar figure for RU 486 when it reaches national distribution. Assuming that half of the current 1.5 million annual abortions in the United States would be requested in the first seven weeks of pregnancy, the methotrexate method would lower the medical bill by at least $250 million.[6]

The pressing issue is what effect the quick success of methotrexate will have on RU 486. Although RU 486 is considered the superior drug by most experts, women may not worry about scientific differences. The biggest factor may well be which drug is first to become widely accessible. Women may, however, be influenced by the ease with which RU 486 is administered as a pill. Doctors say women prefer an oral medication to an injection. A lot may depend on price, too. Methotrexate's low cost may give it an early advantage, but its long-range contribution may be to force down the price of RU 486.

Methotrexate may be hindered early on because relatively few doctors may be willing to administer it. Although FDA-approved for other uses, methotrexate remains experimental as an abortifacient. Drs. Creinin and Schaff have sought to improve its status by securing an Investigative New Drug (IND) license from the FDA, the first step in the official approval process that would eventually allow national marketing. As methotrexate clears each step toward FDA approval, an increasing number of doctors should be recommending it to their patients.

Dr. Hausknecht, too, seeking the imprimatur of major teaching hospitals, has recruited doctors at Columbia University's College of Physicians and Surgeons, Mt. Sinai, and other prominent New York medical centers to initiate their own research projects and apply for an IND from the FDA. Consequently, methotrexate could be administered to as many as two thousand women by the end of 1995.

Although methotrexate research is too new to assess the possible risks that could show up five years hence, the drug's immediate availability puts it in a favorable position relative to RU 486. Only the "made for America" RU 486 being produced by Abortion Rights Mobilization, will be offered to three thousand or more women by the fall of 1995. The Population Council's "made for America" pill is not scheduled for nationwide distribution until a year later. There is a time gap here crying to be filled. For women requesting a medical rather than surgical abortion in 1995 and 1996, methotrexate may answer a critical need. Beyond that, moreover, it offers not a competition between two drugs, but an advantageous choice for women. Doctors could be in the enviable position of being able to recommend one medication over the other to their patients. Women may have a preference when both methods are described to them. As doctors learn the characteristics of each, they will be more likely to administer either drug in the privacy of their offices. And this is the crux of the solution to the abortion crisis; the right of a woman to as much privacy in selecting her abortion as she has in taking an antibiotic or any other drug.

NOTES

1. See five studies by Dr. J. B. Thiersch in Lawrence Lader, *Abortion*, Bobbs-Merrill, New York, 1966, p. 194, fn. 4.

2. Mitchell D. Creinin, A. Eugene Washington, "Cost of Ectopic Pregnancy Management," *Fertility & Sterility*, vol. 60, no. 6, December 1993, pp. 963–69.

3. Mitchell D. Creinin, Philip D. Darney, "Methotrexate and Misoprostol for Early Abortion," *Contraception*, 48, October 1993, pp. 339–47.

4. Mitchell D. Creinin, Eric Vittinghoff, "Methotrexate and Misoprostol vs. Misoprostol Alone for Early Abortion," *Journal of the American Medical Association*, October 19, 1994, vol. 272, no. 15, pp. 1190–95.

5. Eric A. Schaff et al., "Methotrexate for Early Induced Abortion," November 2, 1994 (unpublished), pp. 17–18.

6. Schaff, op. cit., p. 13; Schaff et al., "Protocol to Study Methotrexate for Early Induced Abortion," submitted to FDA, December 22, 1994 (unpublished), pp. 17–18.

In addition to above citations, see Mitchell D. Creinin, "Methotrexate for Abortion at ≤ 42 days Gestation," *Contraception*, 48, December 1993, pp. 519–25; Creinin and David Grimes, "Medical Options for Early Abortion," *Contemporary Ob-Gyn*, April 1994, pp. 85–88; author's interviews by phone with Richard Hausknecht and Eric Schaff.

16

More Clinic Deaths

The ultimate violence came to Boston on December 30, 1994. It chilled the city and horrified the country. The abortion rights movement was now convinced that no clinic anywhere was immune from an assassin's bullets. Around 10 A.M., witnesses reported seeing John Salvi rush into the Planned Parenthood clinic at 1031 Beacon Street firing a .22-caliber rifle. Moments later, a twenty-six-year-old receptionist, Sharon Lowney, lay dying in a pool of blood.

"She was hardly breathing. She was gurgling. She was unconscious," recalled a clinic doctor who had run to her side. "It's horrible when someone dies in your hands, and you can do nothing to help. She died so quickly. She died in my hands."[1]

Then Salvi allegedly raced to a second clinic and committed a second murder. The terror and immediacy rang through Ellen Goodman's column in the *Boston Globe* the next day. The killing site was "only two minutes from my front door." It happened in a building "I know well from endless visits to my child's orthodontist." Boston had always seemed so different from Pensacola, Florida, a safe, civilized city graced by Har-

215

vard, the Massachusetts Institute of Technology, and other top-ranked universities. In Boston, there had been no record of firebombing or similar violence that had long turned Pensacola into a cauldron of fear. Neither Salvi nor any demonstrator around the clinics had ever been rated by the police as a dangerous risk. Yet Richard Seron, a guard at Preterm Health Services, the second clinic to be hit, reported that he saw Salvi on picket lines a month before the killings.[2]

At about 10:20 A.M. that morning, Seron was working in the stockroom just off the clinic's foyer when he heard shots. He rushed to the stockroom door, pulling out his pistol. Leann Nichols, the thirty-eight-year-old receptionist, who was sitting at her desk twelve feet from the front door, now lay dead on the floor. Within moments, Seron said he was exchanging shots with Salvi and was wounded and bloody himself.

The Boston killings raised disturbing questions. When Salvi allegedly came out of the frigid, December air and rang the Planned Parenthood clinic buzzer, why was there no request for identification over the intercom? When he was admitted into the reception area, and began shooting "with quiet, methodical detachment," as the *Globe* described it, why was there no armed guard in the area? The killings and bombings elsewhere in the country seemed to have been ignored. The entry room was "really open and vulnerable," Sarah Judson, a former Planned Parenthood staff member, commented later.[3]

When Salvi allegedly drove his black Toyota pick-up truck a mile away from the Planned Parenthood clinic—he couldn't have run in that brief time—to the Preterm clinic at 1842 Beacon St., the clinic's chief of security, Albie X (most staff members no longer use their last names), was at a nearby stairwell.

Seron was in the stockroom when Salvi was allegedly buzzed in.

A critical question focuses on the role of the Brookline police, both clinics being in this wealthy suburb just over the Boston line to the southwest. When the first emergency call after the Planned Parenthood killing was received at headquarters, why weren't police cars immediately sent to Preterm and other clinics in the area to protect them? At least a warning phone call could have been made to Preterm. For years during the hundreds of arrests of violent demonstrators at these clinics, some officers had called this duty "the baby-killing detail." But this attitude had changed radically. They were no longer considered abortion centers. "They're women's health centers," one lieutenant concluded.[4]

Whatever unstable, tormented elements made up Salvi's personality, he seemed to have planned his assaults scrupulously. He had bought his rifle and handgun long before. He obviously knew the locations of the clinics. "The evidence will, quite obviously, show that these were deliberate, premeditated murders, committed with extreme atrocity and cruelty," John Kivlin, the first assistant district attorney, told the Brookline court.

Another critical question is why Salvi then allegedly undertook a drive of at least twelve hours to pour gunfire into the lobby of the Hillcrest Clinic in Norfolk, Virginia. Along his route, Salvi ignored scores of clinics that might have been attacked. What drew him to Hillcrest, which had long been a target of Virginia fanatics, particularly Rev. Donald Spitz? Spitz's violent clinic demonstrations were notorious. Would someone as unstable and unsophisticated as Salvi have the mental concentration for such planning? The possibility that this third link in his chain of attacks had been guided by a controlling agent, and was part of a planned conspiracy, cannot be ignored.

The anti-abortionists constantly called the Pensacola and Boston killings an aberration coming from "deranged individuals." But columnist Ellen Goodman demanded, "How many deranged individuals does it finally take to make a conspiracy?" After Salvi's capture in Virginia, the question comes into particular focus when Spitz stood outside the jail and shouted through his bullhorn: "Thanks for saving innocent babies from being put to death."[5]

When I arrived at Preterm Health Services in early February 1995, a stooped and grizzled demonstrator was standing on the sidewalk, counting his beads, and seemingly mumbling prayers. A guard checked me at the building door, another at the clinic entrance. Preterm, founded in 1972, is the largest non-profit, tax deductible, reproductive health service in New England. It provides everything from voluntary sterilization to Norplant implants, the "morning after" pill, and treatment for sexually transmitted diseases. Its executive director, Ann F. Osborne, a graduate of the University of Vermont with a masters degree from Northeastern University, has strong, sculptured features and striking blue eyes and blonde hair. She was in Puerto Rico the morning of the killings, but arrived back by plane at 2:30 P.M., rushed from the airfield by a police car.

Richard Seron is a particularly qualified guard. Six feet tall and weighing over two hundred pounds, with dark brown hair and intense brown eyes, he graduated from Boston College and Boston College Law School, and he owns the Armed Personnel Defense Training company. On the morning of the killings, Seron was armed with a Makarov pistol, a Russian gun made in East Germany that holds eight rounds. He is left-handed and carries the weapon on the left side of his belt. Seron reported that the moment Salvi started shooting, he knew it was a .22-caliber rifle, probably being fired with two hands, and heard Nichols crying, "No, no!" in a high-pitched wail.[6]

By the time Seron reached the door of the stockroom, which opens inward with hinges on the right, Nichols was on the floor. He saw Jane Sauer, a twenty-nine-year-old clerk, standing at the copying machine to the right of the entry door. The foyer is shaped like an L, and Sauer was standing in its short wing, trying desperately to hide behind a support column and get some protection from the gunman. Seron reported:

> The gunman's eyes were glazed . . . He had black hair and dark, full eyebrows and a thin mustache. He looked like the devil himself.
>
> He got off one shot at me . . . I got off at least one shot myself and pulled back inside the door. The gunman was trapped momentarily. He was on my right, taking cover from me, but if he wanted to open the front door to escape, he had to take one hand from his rifle, which needed two hands for accuracy.
>
> I moved into the door again, and he sprayed me with bullets. I was hit in the right shoulder, and the doctors haven't removed that bullet yet. I heard the gunman mutter some religious oath, something like "In the name of the mother of God." I tried to fire around the door frame. There must have been at least eight shots between us by now. I got one or two shots through the palm of my left hand, and the number four

knuckle was bleeding badly. I think I got off two more shots, and waited for him. He couldn't have had many bullets left. I could see his bag on the floor near the entry door, and it was lucky I made him abandon it because it had the receipts the police used to identify him.

Seron was bleeding heavily now. "I had to use my right hand to stop the flow in my left hand. My right hand was glued by blood to the wounds and my left hand was glued by blood to the pistol barrel. When the gunman rushed out the entry door, I didn't pursue him. I figured there might be accomplices outside, and the important thing was to protect all the staff members nearby on the floor, so I bolted the entry door quickly." Witnesses said that Salvi kept firing on the street outside, and shells were found later all over the sidewalk. Fortunately, he hit no one, but, ironically, he put a bullet hole through the window of a gray car that bore an anti-abortion sticker on its bumper.

"There is no doubt in my mind," explains Sue K., a Preterm official, "that if Richard had not distracted the gunman with his shots, everyone on that floor of the clinic would be dead." Sue K., whose great aunt, Dr. Sarah Kelman, was a pioneer in the birth control movement, has had long public relations experience in Boston hospitals. Her office is down the hall at least sixty feet from the entry foyer.

I was talking on the phone when I heard some indefinable noise. I shouted to a woman nearby, "What's going on?" I saw Marie running down the hall to the back door. Then I heard shots and screams and called the police. My hand was shaking so badly I could hardly hold the phone. I kept shouting to people down the hall to hide.

Meanwhile, Albie, the security chief, who was on the stairwell, had pressed the code button that shut off other clinic floors, where doctors and patients were located, from the office floor. When the emergency crew arrived, they kept trying C.P.R. on Nichols, but there was no pulse left. "She was a wonderful administrative coordinator," Ann Osborne remembers. "She was shy, almost timid, a person out of the fifties, always feeding animals at animal shelters, living in a tiny cabin in rural New Hampshire."

"What made me feel so awful, what made me feel the saddest," said Sue K., weeping, "was that no one was with Leann when she died. No one was there to hold her hand. She was all alone." Now there is a permanent wreath hanging behind Nichols's desk, saying, "This woman was full of good works."

Osborne flew out to Ohio, protected by a security guard, to attend the Nichols funeral. Leann Nichols's mother said about Salvi: "If they should put him before me, I would shoot him myself."[7]

Despite treatment by a crisis response team of psychiatrists and psychologists from Beth Israel hospital, the Preterm Health Services clinic was in a state of shock for weeks. Many of the staff members suffered from depression, could not focus on their work and could not sleep at night. "I would start crying unexpectedly during the day or night," Sue K. explains. Osborne agreed to be interviewed, with her face showing on ABC's "Prime Time Live" show with Sam Donaldson on January 4th. She immediately got death threats. A clinic staff member was followed home by one anti-abortion demonstrator; after the demonstrator picketed outside her house, she resigned in fear. One woman doctor described walking to and from her car to the clinic: "That was really scary, but I refused to quit." In fact, of sixty-seven staff members, only two have resigned.

When the clinic reopened after three weeks of repairs, a few patients were nervous about keeping appointments. "I'm scared. I haven't decided if I'm going," one said. "The shootings have made me more fervent to go on with our work," Osborne insists. Although the closing put a serious dent in clinic finances, Preterm's patient schedule is now fully booked for weeks.

The police had to break down walls and doors in the entry foyer to recover the bullets. But when I looked over the room in February, the rugs had been cleaned of blood, and the walls had been plastered and repainted. In the mail slots on the wall across from Nichols's desk, however, there are still two bullet holes in the metal.

Secretary of Health and Human Services Donna Shalala quickly visited the clinic, hugging many of the staff members. Although the clinic repeatedly begged U.S. Attorney General Janet Reno for protection, a state police car sits at the front door, but no federal marshals have appeared.

Reno obviously considers Pensacola more vulnerable than Boston. The fanatics think differently. When a Florida jury recommended a possible death sentence for Paul Hill, a Houston anti-abortion leader named Daniel Ware warned that if Hill were executed, "Blood will run in the streets like nobody has ever seen."[8]

NOTES

1. *New York Times,* December 31, 1994, p. A1.
2. Author's interview by phone with Richard Seron.
3. *New York Times,* December 31, 1994, p. A8; *Boston Globe*, December 31, 1994, p. 1.
4. *New York Times,* January 3, 1995, p. A12.
5. Boston *Globe*, January 2, 1995, p. 8.
6. All quotations and narrative from Seron are from author's interview.
7. Author's interview with Ann Osborne; *Boston Globe,* January 2, 1995, p. 9.
8. *New York Times,* January 1, 1995, p. 26.

This chapter is based mainly on interviews with Ann F. Osborne, Richard Seron, and other members of the Preterm Health Services staff who requested anonymity. The officers of the Planned Parenthood clinic declined interviews.

17

The Crisis: 1995

Against a background of clinic killings and bombings, Abortion Rights Mobilization (ARM) worked obsessively in 1995 to bring RU 486 to the American market quickly. The strategy was to relieve pressure on the clinics. If enough doctors administered the abortion pill from their offices, the extremists would have trouble identifying them, invading the premises, or harassing them with picket lines. We would be guaranteeing more privacy for women, and in rural states with only one or two clinics, women could have abortion services much closer to their homes.

The need to introduce RU 486 quickly was pressing. The Republican Congress, led by such fervent anti-abortionists as U.S. Rep. Henry Hyde (R–Illinois), might well attempt to ban RU 486 or put obstacles in its way. There was a quirky desperation about congressional reactions, illustrated by the attacks on Dr. Henry Foster, President Clinton's nominee for U.S. surgeon general, because he may have performed more abortions in his obstetrical-gynecological career than he had acknowledged. ARM's strategy was that if we could get RU 486 accepted quickly and imbedded in the consciousness of the country, legislative attempts to block the pill would become more difficult. Further, we had to prove to American women that the pill was safe and effective. Although we hesitated to pressure our British plant to speed up production of three thousand doses, we were worried that we were falling behind schedule. Dr. David Horne of Columbia University, our chief scientist, remained in constant touch with the British plant to deal with every problem. On May 18, 1995, the British scientist came to Washington, D.C., and we met with the chemist of the Food and Drug Administration (FDA) to check the accuracy of our work so far. We were plagued with mounting costs but still determined to finish production by the fall. Once Dr. Horne had proved through organic chemistry tests that our pill was the exact equivalent of the French abortion pill, and toxicology studies showed it contained no harmful ingredient, we would submit all data to the FDA to get approval for human testing.

Meanwhile, we had put together a high-level medical team to run the tests. Everything would be supervised by Dr. Louise Tyrer, who had been national Planned Parenthood's medical director for sixteen years before retirement. The protocol, or plan, for three test sites had been carefully worked out, calling for a balance between patients at clinics and those at doctors' offices, and a reasonable mix of economic and ethnic backgrounds.

Dr. Eric Schaff, an associate professor at the University of Rochester, had long been in charge of the abortion clinic there and had run trials on methotrexate abortion as well. This would be a unique opportunity to compare the results and women's reactions to RU 486 and methotrexate at the same time. The second test site would be run by Dr. Philip Darney and Dr. Bernard Gore of the University of California, San Francisco General Hospital. They, too, were experienced in the use of methotrexate and would test it along with RU 486, working closely with Steven Heilig, executive director of the San Francisco Medical Society and a long-time ARM ally. The third site would be run by Dr. Antonio Scommegna of the University of Illinois-Chicago.

We were determined to get three thousand tests started in 1995. Their particular importance was speeding up the process by a year. We would use the first "made for America" pills. The Population Council's tests were being run with French pills from the Roussel company. Once the Population Council had used those up, it would have to manufacture its own, which we had already done. The Population Council's target date for national distribution was late 1996, which seemed too far off.

We had told Margaret Catley-Carson, the council's president, that our objective complemented theirs. If they had any problems in manufacturing, we would make the skills of Dr. Horne and our British plant available to them. We wanted to start a national education campaign quickly with our allies, the Feminist Majority and NOW. If the first three thousand tests went smoothly, we would test thousands more. This was allowed under the law with no patent conflict since our project was solely research and produced no profits.

After the Pensacola and Boston killings, ARM searched for every possible strategy to protect the clinics. The immediate danger was that zealots were constantly threatening doctors and staff with bodily harm and even death. Trying to block volunteers from escorting patients into the Park Med clinic in

New York City, John Cain, a rabid demonstrator, shouted, "You're dead! You're all dead." Rev. David Trosch warned Planned Parenthood and NOW officials, "They would be exterminated as vermin is exterminated." At a gas station near the Ladies Center in Pensacola, Florida, a demonstrator threatened, "The place will go up in flames. There will be fireworks."[1]

Such fanatics could eventually resort to assassinations themselves or become the instigators of violence. They were creating a desperate climate around the clinics that was intended to inflame others and could lead to bloodshed. ARM was convinced that these confrontations had to be stopped and began to research a lawsuit as a promising way of doing it.

ARM's possible lawsuit could be brought to federal court under the Freedom of Access to Clinic Entrances (FACE) Act, and possibly under other federal statutes. The lawsuit could be filed in cities where the danger was most acute, or where the defendants were subject to suit. The immediate objective would be to get an injunction from a federal judge that would keep the defendants a reasonable distance from any clinic. But the suit would go beyond that. It would seek to prohibit inflammatory literature from being distributed nationwide, and hopefully put an end to the violence roused by reckless words.

The legal theory behind a potential case is that speech and literature that threaten people's lives are not protected under the First Amendment. A noted precedent came from Justice Oliver Wendell Holmes in a Supreme Court decision that ruled that shouting "fire" in a crowded theater without cause could lead to a disastrous panic, and is not protected speech.[2]

ARM's lawsuit could possibly argue that threats of violence and death, aimed at clinics, doctors, and staff members, are not protected by the First Amendment and should be prohibited. Defendants might also be asked to answer for damages resulting from their inciteful words, including the cost of clinic security already incurred, and that will continue to be incurred when the threats persist. Literature distributed in many states, such as the Army of God's pamphlet urging its members to "destroy at least one death camp" (a clinic), or to eliminate doctors by "removing their hands," would also be encompassed in the suit.

The plaintiffs would probably be clinic directors and staff who have received these threats. Since abortion is only part of most clinics' services, which can range from contraception and sex education to voluntary sterilization, a whole class of women whose health care has been damaged by violence and threats might fall within the plaintiff scope. With the need to increase clinic security intensifying in 1995, ARM hoped to file court papers as soon as possible.*

The task of protecting clinics on a daily basis had become the responsibility of the Feminist Majority under Eleanor Smeal. Its Clinic Access Project, run by Katherine Spillar, has concentrated on the frantic attempts by Operation Rescue and other groups to shut down clinics through turbulent mass demonstrations across the country. The decisive battleground was Los Angeles in 1989, where anti-abortionists swore to close every clinic in the city permanently.

---

*A somewhat similar lawsuit was filed in March 1995 by Dr. David Gunn's family, claiming that John Burt was part of a conspiracy against clinic doctors that instigated Dr. Gunn's assassination.

The Feminist Majority counterattack was based on working with local prochoice forces to recruit volunteers and train them in defensive strategies. These forces were linked by a communications network of cellular phones and two-way radios. On one peak day, almost five thousand volunteers surrounded the city's clinics. In all, ten thousand volunteers were trained for defense duty in the city. When the volunteers outnumbered the demonstrators week after week, and not one clinic closed down, Operation Rescue gave up its attempt to blockade Los Angeles.

The Feminist Majority sent a similar Clinic Defense Team to Buffalo, New York, in 1992, where the mayor had actually invited Operation Rescue to the city. Not one of four clinics was ever shut down, and the blockade was abandoned after a week.[3]

Again in 1994 in Birmingham, Alabama; Jackson, Mississippi; Fort Wayne, Indiana; and other cities, blockades were broken up by a huge outpouring of volunteers. The Feminist Majority had to put special defense efforts into Florida after Operation Rescue moved its "boot camp" to Melbourne to teach its members methods of terrorizing clinics. When Dr. Gunn was murdered, doctors at the Melbourne clinic became so frightened that two quit immediately, and the clinic's survival was in doubt until new doctors could be found. The local police refused to enforce a state-ordered buffer zone despite a State Supreme Court ruling upholding the injunction.[4] In this crisis, particularly in Pensacola, the Feminist Majority adopted a policy of sending defense teams to work right within clinic offices.

It was imperative to keep the Ft. Lauderdale Women's Clinic open. Forty percent of its clients were poor; a quarter of them were Haitians. It was the only facility in the area accepting HIV patients. At the clinic an abortion cost only $210 compared to the national average of $350. Voluntary sterilization for women cost only $650 whereas nearby hospitals charged $2,500 to $5,000. After the Women's Clinic lost its lease in the summer of 1993, the Feminist Majority gave it the money to relocate.

An essential step was the hiring by the Feminist Majority of a well-known international security firm to assess security conditions at twenty vulnerable clinics throughout the nation, and to work with them in strengthening every detail of defense. The Feminist Majority also established an emergency fund to pay for bulletproof vests, video equipment to scan surrounding areas, and more guards when badly needed.

Another aspect of security was the lawsuit brought under the Racketeer Influenced and Corrupt Organizations (RICO) Act against Joseph Scheidler, Randall Terry, and other flagrant violators of clinic and patients' rights. Its aim was to prosecute those who had continually tried to destroy women-owned businesses and property, and cause economic injury as a result of criminal activity. The case had been started when Eleanor Smeal was president of NOW, and the Supreme Court had already ruled that RICO could be applied to the protection of clinics. With Feminist Majority lawyers joining NOW's lawyers, the trial was scheduled for federal court in Chicago once preliminary "discovery" was completed.

In the last year, Eleanor Smeal, Patricia Ireland of NOW, Kate Michelman of NARAL,* Pamela Maraldo of Planned

---

*Name changed to National Abortion and Reproductive Rights Action League

Parenthood Federation, and other movement leaders have increasingly pushed Attorney General Janet Reno to step up government enforcement of clinic security. For twelve years, with Republicans in the White House, the problem had been ignored.

President Bush had even gone to court to deny federal protection for clinics. Now the issue goes deeper than more federal marshals. Smeal insists that the real objective must be to investigate and charge what appears to be a nationwide terrorist conspiracy. The pattern seems relentless and inescapable. Just a month after the Boston killings, a fire destroyed the Planned Parenthood clinic at San Luis Obispo, California. It was the fifth arson attack on clinics in California in less than a month, indicating a carefully conceived plan.[5]

The Justice Department and the FBI claim that they are constantly investigating, yet they have never come up with a shred of evidence of a conspiracy or the money behind it. "The government has refused to take terrorism against women as seriously as it takes the drug war," Smeal concludes. "It treats each killing, each firebombing as an individual act, not a planned assault. It approaches terrorism mainly through politics."[6]

Is Janet Reno responsible for this dilatory approach? Smeal thinks it is the White House itself. "President Clinton refused to make abortion rights an issue in the 1994 elections, preferring to push such things as tax reform and immigration," Smeal observes. "But where is his support coming from if not from women?" Many black voters, another consistent Clinton block, stayed home on election day. Even in liberal states like New York, about half of all eligible women voters ignored prochoice

Democrats and often supported antichoice Republicans. The only possible conclusion is that without the president's emphasis on abortion, women were not confronted with an issue crucial to their lives, and were drawn to such platforms as tax cuts.

It seems difficult to define the factors influencing Clinton, whether intensified prodding from the Catholic hierarchy, a conviction that the middle class is concerned only with lower taxes and a balanced budget, or fear of the vote-getting of the Christian Coalition. Yet figures show the coalition represents only 15 percent of registered Republicans. Gov. William Weld of Massachusetts stresses that it is intellectually dishonest for conservatives to advocate less government "while keeping a foot on individual liberty." "If Clinton ignores his base among women, blacks and labor unions, and hesitates to prosecute clinic terrorists vigorously," Smeal sums up, "he is risking his chances in 1996 and the chances of the Democratic party."

It seemed frightening that the abortion conflict had reached a peak of fury as late as 1995, thirty years after my article in the *New York Times Magazine* had laid down the first constitutional and philosophic arguments for legalization. Essentially, the conflict had never changed. The "core issue," as Rev. Alfred R. Guthrie stressed in a letter to the *Times* of January 16, 1995, was still whether the child/fetus/embryo in the womb is a human being, and whether abortions are, by definition, the elimination of unwanted human beings." Father Guthrie's very choice of words—human being as opposed to person—pinpoints the conflict. While the Catholic church, along with most fundamentalists, bases its stand on the belief that in an abortion a human being has been killed, most Americans, including almost all Protestant and Jewish denominations, believe that the fetus is not a person, particularly in its early development.

This was the position taken by the U.S. Supreme Court in *Roe* v. *Wade.* As to the "difficult question of when life begins," the Court ruled,

> When those trained in the respective disciplines of medicine, philosophy and theology are unable to arrive at any consensus, the judiciary, at this point in the development of man's knowledge, is not in a position to speculate as to the answer.

The Court declared that "the word 'person,' as used in the Fourteenth Amendment, does not include the unborn." The Court, therefore, concluded: "In short, the unborn have never been recognized in the law as persons in the whole sense." At the same time, the Court granted the states a measure of control over abortion. In the first trimester of pregnancy, the decision is left completely to the medical judgment of the woman's doctor. In the second trimester, the Court ruled that a state may regulate the abortion procedure "in ways that are reasonably related to maternal health." In the third trimester, the Court ruled a state may "regulate, and even proscribe, abortion except where it is necessary, in appropriate medical judgment, for the preservation of the life or health of the mother."

While the religious beliefs of Father Guthrie and all anti-abortionists are an accepted part of American diversity, the crux of the continuing conflict is that they have refused to accept the Court's decision on legal personhood as binding. Sensible people on both sides have searched for a way of defusing the differences, and keeping the debate on a rational level. There are those that believe, Justice Ruth Bader Ginsburg, that the furor could have been moderated from the start if other political and legal routes had been followed. Justice Ginsburg contended in a New York University Law School speech on March 9, 1993, that *Roe* v. *Wade's* "muscularity" was "unnecessary." By that, she seemed to have meant that the Court's decision was too sweeping and too far ahead of cautious progress. She claimed that *Roe* v. *Wade* may have "halted a political process that was moving in a reform direction" and thus "prolonged divisiveness and deferred stable settlement of the issue."[7]

Justice Ginsburg's thesis, however, misreads the historical course of events. The abortion clash had escalated long before *Roe* v. *Wade*. Once the National Abortion Rights Action League (NARAL) had decided at its founding meeting in February 1969 that its objective would be total "repeal" of the old, punitive laws, rather than supporting the step-by-step "reform" laws that Justice Ginsburg seems to have favored, the era of half-measures had ended. We knew that only repeal could move the country, and we were right. The movement grew explosively on that platform.

The passage of New York State's repeal law in April 1970 confirmed the momentum for revolutionary change. Although Justice Ginsburg seems to argue that reform laws, such as those passed in 1967 in Colorado and North Carolina, were creating a "stable settlement of the issue," these laws only approved abortion for a handful of women. They were redundant by 1970. A majority of the public was now demanding repeal. A decisive change in national opinion had already destroyed the point of Ginsburg's thesis.

Justice Ginsburg's second argument, that there was an increasing spurt of legislative change before *Roe* v. *Wade,* making a sweeping Court decision unnecessary, also fails to meet reality. New repeal laws were passed in Alaska, Hawaii, and Washington State in 1971. It seems possible that other repeal laws, possibly in California, Illinois, and a handful of other states, might have been passed in the next few years, providing perhaps a dozen centers for abortion rights across the country. But legislative action was difficult and slow. Even if Justice Ginsburg were right, and the gradual passage of state repeal laws could have delayed the shock of *Roe* v. *Wade,* I doubt that the fury of the conflict would have been tempered. The movement was pushing for legalized abortion nationwide. Court challenges to the old laws had been started in a score of states, and one was bound to reach the Supreme Court fairly soon. Admittedly, the Court could have delayed a decision for another five years. Its ruling could also have been more moderate than that set forth in *Roe* v. *Wade.* But I am convinced that once enough states had legalized abortion, the pressure on the Court would have been too great to pull back from nationwide legalization. The clash between abortion rights and anti-abortionists was already too advanced to dilute the opposing interests.

Despite Ginsburg's hesitancy on the timing of *Roe* v. *Wade,* her testimony at her Senate confirmation hearings confirmed her commitment to a woman's choice for abortion. Asked her position on privacy rights, Ginsburg replied,

This is something central to a woman's life, to her dignity. It's a decision she must make for herself. And when government controls that decision for her, she's being treated as something less than a fully adult human responsible for her own choices. . . . The state controlling the woman is both denying her full autonomy and full equality with men.

Historian David Garrow claimed in an op-ed piece in the *New York Times* on January 6, 1995, that the five recent clinic assassinations represent the "death throes of an anti-abortion movement in which almost every remaining participant realizes that the way to overturn *Roe* v. *Wade* has been irretrievably lost." Comparing abortion bloodshed to the civil rights turmoil and Klan killings of the 1960s, he contends that "history shows us, American law can and does put an end to the politics of terrorism."

But what Garrow ignores, unfortunately, is that the whole point of terrorism is to make the law unworkable and virtually nullify it. Killings, bombings, and harassment of clinics have made it increasingly difficult to keep them open and replace doctors and staff members. The extremists may be mentally unbalanced, but their policy is sound. They are waging a war of attrition. The critical stage of abortion rights may depend as much on the courage and staying power of its forces as on the commitment of law enforcement to protect the clinics.

Another element in this crisis is the political influence of the Christian Coalition. No doubt it was pivotal in electing a large percentage of Republican House members in 1994. On February 11, 1995, it called in its chips by announcing it would not support either a Republican presidential or vice presidential candidate in 1996 who was not pledged against abortion. No one knows whether the coalition would have the convention delegates to carry out this threat and block a pro-choice moderate such as Gov. William Weld of Massachusetts. The odds would seem to be on the side of the coalition.

Until 1996 at least, President Clinton's veto and the difficulty of an override in Congress offer reasonable safeguards for abortion rights. If there is an anti-abortion Republican president after that, the prospects are ominous. There are many legislative approaches that could curtail the strength of *Roe* v. *Wade*. Even if such restricting legislation would eventually be deemed unconstitutional by the Supreme Court, judicial relief is a slow process. Anti-abortion legislation could harass women's access to abortion for years.

Curtailment and harassment could possibly be carried out by the executive order of a Republican president. One possibility is that if RU 486 is manufactured overseas for use here, as is likely, the president could force it on the list of prohibited drugs and stop its importation. Another possibility is that the prostaglandin, taken along with RU 486 and made by only one company here, could be so loaded with medical restrictions that the manufacturer would give up production. Such dangers are more than speculative, and they can only be confronted if prochoice political organizing becomes as efficient in 1996 as the Christian Coalition's proved to be in 1994.

Still, I am convinced that historical movements have their own built-in energy. If they are strongly grounded in people's needs and aspirations, such as the movements for abolition of slavery, enfranchisement of women, and the struggle for civil rights, they grow and progress irreversibly. They may be stalled for a time, and channeled briefly in wrong directions. But the force behind them is like a raging flood that can never be halted.

The strength of the women's movement seems to me to tower over two centuries of American progress. It has grappled with the blood of clinic killings, and steeled itself for the possibility of more. It has had to deal with subsidiary issues such as pornography and homosexuality, which are crucial but never central to the overriding quest for procreative rights and women's total control of their bodies. The movement has occasionally become factionalized. The media has often misrepresented it to the public. Yet it has always returned to its primary aims.

Women's anger is the bedrock of the movement. Those who have witnessed the hundreds of thousands, perhaps half a million, marching through Washington, D.C., in 1989 and later demonstrations can hardly underrate the passion behind these turnouts. Women know all too well that their lives and their health are at stake. Their personal achievements, as well as maternal health and the health of any offspring, depend upon control of their childbearing. Anger and passion direct their destiny.

For proof, women have only to consider Rumania and what its people suffered when abortion was made illegal in 1966. Abortion-related maternal deaths rose dramatically from 20 per 1,000 live births in 1965 to between 120 and 150 in the 1982–89 period. Abortion-related deaths as a percentage of deaths from all causes rose from about 20 percent to nearly 90 percent. That rate was ten times higher than for any other European country, all then having legalized abortion. The shocking pictures of abandoned children warehoused and barely surviving in national depositories are a permanent reminder of those punitive years.

It is a mistake to think that religious convictions are only on the side of Catholic and fundamentalist anti-abortionists. Pro-choice groups may not quote from the Bible, but they have their own kind of moral fervor. Whatever their religious denomination, if any, they are driven by an ethical force that seeks to create a more beautiful environment and a range of fulfilling options for the individual. Women want the right of abortion because they care. They care about how a child grows up. They care about coping with the responsibility of child rearing. They know that nothing is more cruel than bringing an unwanted child into the world, and they insist that a child needs parental love.

All these principles were laid down by Margaret Sanger eighty years ago. They are still the basis of the abortion rights movement today. Few people could survive the daily rigors of the women's movement or the family planning movement if they lacked such moral beliefs. They want a better society built case by case, each choice adding to an indestructible right of choice for everyone. This is one of the essential moral visions of our time. Abortion rights is a creative, forward-moving process. Its opponents want a static and restrictive prison with women as its victims. There is no doubt in my mind that clinic defense and the introduction of RU 486 into the United States, despite its strategic and financial risks, will be the coming battleground. Reason and dedication will carry abortion rights through to the next century and beyond.

NOTES

1. Evidence in the files of ARM attorneys.

2. *Schenck* v. *United States,* 249 U.S. 47 (1919).

3. Feminist Majority Foundation, Arlington, Virginia, "National Clinic Access Project," February 4, 1994, p. 8.

4. Feminist Majority Foundation, "National Clinic Access Project," February 4, 1994, pp. 4–5.

5. *New York Times,* March 3, 1995, p. A16.

6. Author's interview with Eleanor Smeal in this and following paragraphs.

7. *New York Times,* July 22, 1993, p. A20.

Appendix

PUBLIC LAW 103–259

103rd Congress—2nd Session

S. 636

103 P.L. 259; 108 Stat. 694
1994 Enacted S. 636; 103 Enacted S. 636

SYNOPSIS:

An Act

To amend title 18, United States Code, to assure freedom of access to reproductive services.

May 26, 1994—PUBLIC LAW 103–259

TEXT:

Be it enacted by the Senate and House of Representatives of the United States of America in Congress assembled,

[*1] SECTION 1. SHORT TITLE.

This Act may be cited as the "Freedom of Access to Clinic Entrances Act of 1994".

[*2] SECTION 2. PURPOSE.

Pursuant to the affirmative power of Congress to enact this legislation under section 8 of article I of the Constitution, as well as under section 5 of the fourteenth amendment to the Constitution, it is the purpose of this Act to protect and promote the public safety and health and activities affecting interstate commerce by establishing Federal criminal penalties and civil remedies for certain violent, threatening, obstructive and destructive conduct that is intended to injure, intimidate or interfere with persons seeking to obtain or provide reproductive health services.

[*3] SEC. 3. FREEDOM OF ACCESS TO CLINIC ENTRANCES.

Chapter 13 of title 18, United States Code, is amended by adding at the end thereof the following new section:

[*248] Freedom of Access to Clinic Entrances "248 Freedom of Access to Clinic Entrances.

"(a) Prohibited Activities.—Whoever—

"(1) by force or threat of force or by physical obstruction, intentionally injures, intimidates or interferes with or attempts to injure, intimidate or interfere with any person because that person is or has been, or in order to intimidate such person or any other person or any class of persons from, obtaining or providing reproductive health services;

"(2) by force or threat of force or by physical obstruction, intentionally injures, intimidates or interferes with or attempts to injure, intimidate or interfere with any person lawfully exercising or seeking to exercise the First Amendment right of religious freedom at a place of religious worship; or

"(3) intentionally damages or destroys the property of a facility, or attempts to do so, because such facility provides reproductive health services, or intentionally damages or destroys the property of a place of religious worship, shall be subject to the penalties provided in subsection (b) and the civil remedies provided in subsection (c), except that a parent or legal guardian of a minor shall not be subject to any penalties or civil remedies under this section for such activities insofar as they are directed exclusively at that minor.

"(b) Penalties.—Whoever violates this section shall—

"(1) in the case of a first offense, be fined in accordance with this title, or imprisoned not more than one year, or both; and

"(2) in the case of a second or subsequent offense after a prior conviction under this section, be fined in accordance with this title, or imprisoned not more than 3 years, or both; except that for an offense involving exclusively a nonviolent physical obstruction, the fine shall be not more than $10,000 and the length of imprisonment shall be not more than six months, or both, for the first offense; and the fine shall be not more than $25,000 and the length of imprisonment shall be not more than 18 months, or both, for a subsequent offense; and except that if bodily injury results, the length of imprisonment shall be not more than 10 years, and if death results, it shall be for any term of years or for life.

"(c) Civil Remedies.—

"(1) Right of action.—

"(A) In general.—Any person aggrieved by reason of the conduct prohibited by subsection (a) may commence a civil action for the relief set forth in subparagraph (B), except that such an action may be brought under subsection (a) (1) only by a person involved in providing or seeking to provide, or obtaining or seeking to obtain, services in a facility that provides reproductive health services, and such an action may be brought under subsection (a) (2) only by a person lawfully exercising or seeking to exercise the First Amendment right of religious freedom at a place of religious worship or by the entity that owns or operates such place of religious worship.

"(B) Relief.—In any action under subparagraph (A), the court may award appropriate relief, including temporary, preliminary or permanent injunctive relief and compensatory and punitive damages, as well as the costs of suit and reasonable fees for attorneys and expert witnesses. With respect to compensatory damages, the plaintiff may elect, at any time prior to the rendering of final judgment, to recover, in lieu of actual damages, an award of statutory damages in the amount of $5,000 per violation.

"(2) Action by attorney general of the United States.—
"(A) In general.—If the Attorney General of the United States has reasonable cause to believe that any person or group of persons is being, has been, or may be injured by conduct constituting a violation of this section, the Attorney General may commence a civil action in any appropriate United States District Court.
"(B) Relief.—In any action under subparagraph (A), the court may award appropriate relief, including temporary, preliminary or permanent injunctive relief, and compensatory damages to persons aggrieved as described in paragraph (1) (B). The court, to vindicate the public interest, may also assess a civil penalty against each respondent—
"(i) in an amount not exceeding $10,000 for a nonviolent physical obstruction and $15,000 for other first violations; and
"(ii) in an amount not exceeding $15,000 for a nonviolent physical obstruction and $25,000 for any other subsequent violation.

"(3) Actions by State attorney general.—
"(A) In general.—If the Attorney General of a State has reasonable cause to believe that any person or group of persons is being, has been, or may be injured by conduct constituting a violation of this section, such Attorney General may commence a civil action in the name of such State, as parens patriae on behalf of natural persons residing in such State, in any appropriate United States District Court.
"(B) Relief.—In any action under subparagraph (A), the court

may award appropriate relief, including temporary, preliminary or permanent injunctive relief, compensatory damages, and civil penalties as described in paragraph (2) (B).

"(d) Rules of Construction.—Nothing in this section shall be construed—

"(1) to prohibit any expressive conduct (including peaceful picketing or other peaceful demonstration) protected from legal prohibition by the First Amendment to the Constitution;

"(2) to create new remedies for interference with activities protected by the free speech or free exercise clauses of the First Amendment to the Constitution, occurring outside a facility, regardless of the point of view expressed, or to limit any existing legal remedies for such interference;

"(3) to provide exclusive criminal penalties or civil remedies with respect to the conduct prohibited by this section, or to preempt State or local laws that may provide such penalties or remedies; or

"(4) to interfere with the enforcement of State or local laws regulating the performance of abortions or other reproductive health services.

"(e) Definitions.—As used in this section:

"(1) Facility.—The term 'facility' includes a hospital, clinic, physician's office, or other facility that provides reproductive health services, and includes the building or structure in which the facility is located.

"(2) Interfere with.—The term 'interfere with' means to restrict a person's freedom of movement.

"(3) Intimidate.—The term 'intimidate' means to place a person in reasonable apprehension of bodily harm to him- or herself or to another.

"(4) Physical obstruction.—The term 'physical obstruction' means rendering impassable ingress to or egress from a facility that provides reproductive health services or to or from a place of religious worship, or rendering passage to or from such a facility or place of religious worship unreasonably difficult or hazardous.

"(5) Reproductive health services.—The term 'reproductive health services' means reproductive health services provided in a hospital, clinic, physician's office, or other facility, and includes medical, surgical, counselling or referral services relating to the human reproductive system, including services relating to pregnancy or the termination of a pregnancy.

"(6) State.—The term 'State' includes a State of the United States, the District of Columbia, and any commonwealth, territory, or possession of the United States."

[*4] SEC. 4. CLERICAL AMENDMENT.

The table of sections at the beginning of chapter 13 of title 18, United States Code, is amended by adding at the end the following new item: "248. Blocking access to reproductive health services."

[*5] SEC. 5. SEVERABILITY.

If any provision of this Act, an amendment made by this Act, or the application of such provision or amendment to any person or circumstances is held to be unconstitutional, the remainder of this Act, the amendments made by this Act, and the application of the provision of such to any other person or circumstance shall not be affected thereby.

[*6] SEC. 6. EFFECTIVE DATE.

This Act takes effect on the date of the enactment of this Act, and shall apply only with respect to conduct occurring on or after such date.

Speaker of the House of Representatives.
Vice President of the United States and President of the Senate.

Acknowledgments

My debt to my wife, Joan Summers Lader, seems to grow with each book. Her help on research, editing, and interpretation of the abortion rights movement, in which she was an important partner, can hardly be measured. I also owe much to our daughter, Wendy Summers Lader, for her love and support.

I have been with my agent, Roberta Pryor, for over thirty years, and still marvel at her hard work and kindness.

Because this is a personal book of my involvement with abortion rights since my first writing about it in 1962, much of it comes from memory. I have also drawn often on my personal papers, letters, and documents, both those on deposit in the manuscript division of the New York Public Library and those still in my possession.

I am indebted to many interviews given by sources essential to the coverage of the growing abortion violence, particularly in Pensacola and Boston. Most of these, except for people requesting anonymity, are cited in the notes at the end of each chapter. I must thank above all for their constant help Eleanor Smeal, president of the Feminist Majority Foundation, and her staff, including Jennifer Jackman, Caroline Tesche, and Katherine Spillar.

Stanley Henshaw and Michael Klitsch of the Alan Guttmacher Institute have always given me the best of their counsel and research.

For scientific accuracy, I depend frequently on Dr. David Horne of the Columbia University Chemistry Department, Dr. Eric Schaff of the University of Rochester, and Steven Heilig of the San Francisco Medical Society. Five lawyers have been invaluable: Milton Bass, Marshall Beil, Edward Costikyan, Jesse Rothstein, and Maria Vullo.

My special appreciation to my editor, Steven L. Mitchell, for his encouragement and diligence.

Index

The Author

Lawrence Lader has long been recognized as the pioneering writer on abortion rights and family planning in the country. His biography of Margaret Sanger was published in 1955. His 1966 book, *Abortion*—the first to advocate a woman's total control over her reproductive life—opened a national debate on one of the most controversial issues of our time and was cited often in *Roe* v. *Wade,* the U.S. Supreme Court decision legalizing abortion. Lader was presented with the National Organization for Women's Certificate of Distinction for "Outstanding Leadership for Women's Rights" in April 1989 and the Feminist Majority Foundation award of "Feminist of the Year" 1992.

A founding chair of the National Abortion Rights Action League (1969–1975), Lader helped put together the campaign producing the landmark New York State law of 1970. Since 1975 he has been president of Abortion Rights Mobilization.

A former adjunct associate professor in New York University's school of journalism and former president of the American Society of Authors and Journalists, Lader has written more than 450 articles for *American Heritage, Collier's, New York Times Magazine, New Republic,* and other national magazines. He is married to Joan Summers Lader, a former opera singer.